Working

A Beginner's Guide To Accessing
And Working With Natural
Energy Forces

Shirley O Donoghue

Working With Natural Energy

Cover design by Paul Mason

Published by:

Capall Bann Publishing
Freshfields
Chieveley
Berks
RG20 8TF

Contents

About the author

Shirley O'Donoghue is a Crystal Healer who has been teaching Psychic Awareness courses in various locations including Adult Education Colleges, Complementary Therapy Centres etc. as well as writing magazine articles on Crystal therapy. She runs her own College, the Lucis College of Crystal Therapy which trains to practitioner level.

She is developing a range of meditation tapes and also a range of essential oils linked with crystals.

She has appeared on Sky TV and also various radio stations to discuss the beneficial effects that crystals can impart.

In addition to the above she runs a thriving healing practice. She is married with 3 sons.

Shirley's website address is www.lucisgroup.com

Introduction

The idea to put down on paper what has gradually evolved over the last 3 years of working as a teacher of something euphemistically known as 'Psychic Studies', has been an idea which I have thought about a rejected. But through the group work that I have been privileged to be a part of, I have gradually started to accept that it is time now for people to start to access again the energies which I am sure were once a part of everyday life for our ancestors.

In the hustle and bustle of our busy lives we have lost the ability to 'tune into' these energies and to work with them. This ability can be remembered with a little time, patience and open-mindedness on the part of the person wishing to gain a greater understanding of a world which really exists.

A few years ago I decided to learn to meditate in order purely to achieve a relaxed state of mind. I had three boys with only a year's gap in between each of them and life was pretty hectic and demanding! As the process of meditation began to slowly evolve for me I discovered that in taking time out from the busy pace of life, I became sensitive to other energies around me that were there. This was an exciting and joyful time for me as I found a process of unfoldment taking place.

For my husband and sons, there was a period of adaptation, as they saw the level headed person slowly change into someone whose perceptions and experiences would, by many, have been seen as away with the fairies! They have been a great anchor and support to me over this time. Encouraging and being open to sharing the knowledge that I started to gain, I could not have progressed without their love and understanding.

In this book, I hope to show practical ways to experience the energies and effects that they can engender. It is my opinion that within the exercises that are presented, lie keys to knowledge which will enable you to begin to heal and enhance your understanding of life and how to live it to the best of your ability.

1. Basic Guide to Getting Started

When connecting with natural energies, it is important to develop the ability to be able to "tune in"î to these energies in order to facilitate awareness of them. The most basic way to do this is to begin to learn to meditate.

The brain is divided into two sections or hemispheres - left and right. Some people acknowledge that the right side is related to female traits such as intuition, musical and artistic appreciation in addition to controlling the functions of the left side of the body, whilst the left or male side controls logic and practical thinking as well as the right side of the body. Research has shown that meditation allows the two different sides to merge and communicate allowing for balance in thought processes between each hemisphere.

The activity within the brain can be measured by a process using an EEG (electroencephalograph) machine that measures the electrical activity of the brain. This activity is broken down into four categories or Brain Rhythms: Beta, Alpha, Theta and Delta

WAKING STATE - BETA (13-30 Hz)

DREAM STATE - ALPHA (8-13 Hz)

DEEP MEDITATION - THETA (4-7 Hz)

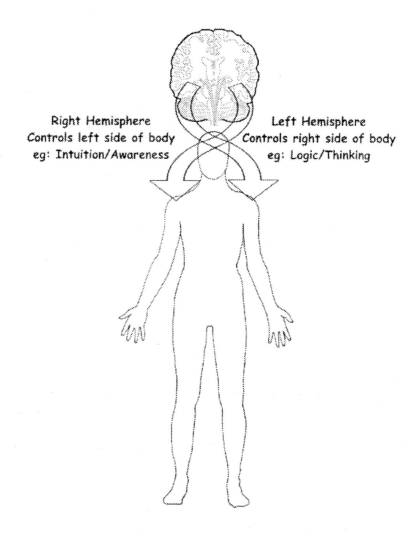

Right Hemisphere
Controls left side of body
eg: Intuition/Awareness

Left Hemisphere
Controls right side of body
eg: Logic/Thinking

LEFT AND RIGHT BRAIN-BODY ASSOCIATION

DIAGRAM 1 - Brain functions

DEEP SLEEP - DELTA (0.5-4 Hz)

Meditation allows the mind to slow the brain rhythms, which stops the conscious thoughts and this in turn lets the subconscious thoughts filter through. People vary in their opinion as to whether it is inspired thoughts that come from a divine source or whether it is merely another part of the human psyche that has been accessed. However most people do agree that meditation is extremely beneficial in reducing stress, aiding relaxation, and reducing anxiety.

Once mastered (and this is not as difficult as people imagine), meditation can provide a 'quick fix' in stressful situations. For example when one is faced with a high workload, 5 minutes of meditation will centre the person and provide focus so that they are able to concentrate more fully on what needs to be done.

A simple meditative exercise to help reduce stress would be to work with the breath. The breath acts as a focus that enables the body to harness the physical and mental responses to stress and alleviate the adverse conditions that arise. It also has a positive chemical effect when done correctly as deep breathing allows nutrients and oxygen to be taken into the lungs, lower diaphragm and abdomen. These are key places where tension can be held and the process of deep, regular breathing allows for the release of this tension.

Exercise: Counting The Breaths

An extremely effective yet simple form of meditation which enables you to begin to harness the mind. Sit in a comfortable position with your eyes closed. Try to relax any points of tension that you hold in the body that you are aware of.
Inhale and exhale and count "one", be aware of the complete process and repeat counting "two" then again counting "three"

until you reach the count of "ten". To start with you might find it difficult to get to "two"! But persevere, if your mind wanders return to the process from "one" again. After 15 minutes or so you will find that you have become more centered and calm, enabling you to focus more clearly on whatever you wish to do.

Meditation is best learned in a group situation as there is much to be gained with the mutual exchange of experiences had during meditating. Some things that are dismissed as imagination such specific sensations within the body, an ability to 'see' colours in the mind's eye and so on are more easily accepted and explored when it can be discussed with others in conjunction with an experienced teacher.

When preparing to meditate it is best to do so in comfortable, warm surroundings. Wear loose fitting clothing and try not to eat directly before meditation. You may find that you fall asleep sometimes so it is obviously best to ensure that you do not need to jump up and rush anywhere after meditating. Time your meditation to last anything between 20 minutes to 1 hour to begin with. As with exercise you may find that you have 'good' and 'bad' days - it will pay to persevere.

Transcendental Meditation (TM) is a form of meditation popularized by the Beatles and other well-known personalities of the sixties. Mental activity is reduced and a meditative state achieved by using a Mantra as a meditation aid. A Mantra being a special word or series of words which are chanted or repeated over and over until the state of mind changes. A Mantra is considered to be special to the person using it and should not be given freely to others. It can be a verse or simply one word such as 'love' repeated over and over again.

Guided Meditations are currently gaining in popularity and there is a vast amount of pre-recorded tapes which you can buy offering specific meditations to cover things from weight loss, low self esteem to connecting with your Higher Self.

The mind can have an extremely powerful effect upon the physical body. A good experiment is to read the following passage through:

"Imagine a lemon. Pick it up and hold it in your hand. Bring the lemon to your nose and smell the fresh aroma. Look at the yellow skin and pierce it with your fingernail. Smell the stronger aroma as the lemon oil is released from the skin. Take a knife and cut the lemon in half cutting a slice and placing it in your mouth."

Having read the passage above it is a sure bet that you will find that your mouth at some point started to water. If reading a few words on paper can have such a powerful effect what can emotions like worry, guilt and anger do to the physical body?

Use meditation time as a gift to yourself from you. Value this time and do not regard it as an indulgence but more as a way of maintaining an emotional, spiritual, mental and physical equilibrium which strengthens your body against the stresses and strains of everyday life.

Before you meditate a pleasant 'ritual' is to light a candle and burn incense or essential oils. You may wish to play some relaxing music and some specialist outlets have particular meditation music which can specifically work in slowing down the brain waves to help achieve a meditative state. You may prefer to meditate at the same time each day, in the same place or position with the same aromas from oils or incense. All of this routine helps to get the mind to "switch" into the right mental channels and attune you more quickly to the most receptive brain waves, thereby making the whole process easier to achieve and therefore more effective.

Exercíse To Work Wíth The Chakras

The following is a meditation to open the chakras which are the energetic gateways of the body. For more information on the chakras, refer to Chapter 3 in this book). You may wish to record the meditation on tape before actually starting as this will help you to remember the processes involved.

Sit comfortably ensuring that you are warm (during meditation the temperature of the body tends to drop).

Breathe in deeply and sigh out 3 times.

Take your awareness to the Crown Chakra situated at the top of your head, Visualise a light from high above the Crown and draw a strand of this light in through the Crown Chakra. As the light enters the Crown become aware of the centre starting to expand and draw more light in. As you allow this light to fill up the centre visualise it continuing to flow down into the Brow Chakra.

At the Brow Chakra feel the light passing into the centre opening it up and 'flushing through' any blocked energy. See it becoming more open and energised and allow the light to flow on into the Throat Chakra.

Again see the Throat Chakra expanding and as it expands see any blockages being cleared. As the light flows through the centre it re-balances and continues its flow into the Heart Chakra.

At the Heart Chakra see the light begin to clear debris and blockages as it fills up this centre. Try to get a sense of expansion of energy and see the light flowing into the Solar Plexus Chakra.

The Solar Plexus is the energetic mouth of the body so at this point take in 3 deep breaths through the Solar Plexus and be

8

aware of prana, chi or life-force energy being carried throughout the body via the meridians. Once this is done take your focus back to the Solar Plexus and again see the light filling this centre until it expands, clearing any debris or blockages. Continuing its flow into the Sacral Chakra.

Allow the Sacral to take in the light as it fills, see or become aware of the light flushing through the whole of the chakra before it finally passes into the Base Chakra. Again see the light filling up the Base Chakra and clearing any blockages. As this centre becomes expanded, be aware of the energy flowing down your legs and ankles and out through the soles of your feet into the earth where it links to a rock, tree root or crystal which anchors and grounds the light.

Take your awareness to the whole of the chakra system and 'see' yourself as a column of light in which each cell is vibrating in perfect harmony. Send more light to any chakra or part of you which is still out of balance and when you are ready bring your awareness back into the room, feeling the weight of your body on the chair and your feet firmly on the ground. Breathing more deeply, in your own time and when you are ready, open your eyes.

Many types of Yoga incorporate meditation within their discipline as does Tai Chi and other eastern forms of exercise which are now gaining in popularity and acceptance. There are usually many classes available in these subjects at Adult Education Colleges at very reasonable rates as well as many private teachers and schools. When selecting your course, it is always a good idea to ensure that the person teaching you is properly qualified. This can be established by asking the college or tutor about their qualifications and experience and contacting relevant governing bodies to the therapies which you are seeking to learn to check on their requirements for membership.

At its very basic level, meditation will enable you to become more relaxed and focussed quickly and easily. On the other hand it can open up another level of understanding in terms of self-knowledge and spirituality.

As you develop and grow in your awareness, you may find that you become more empathic in social situations, sensing undercurrents of emotions for example. Illustrations of this may be that you find that you are aware if a couple have had an argument even they are going to great lengths to cover the disagreement up. You may pick up on someone's underlying feelings and find that you are able to sympathise with them strongly.

As my abilities began to develop I became very aware of this when I was taken to a pop concert which I was extremely reluctant to go to. The tickets were a birthday gift, it was a cold winter's night, raining, I was extremely tired and we were late and had trouble parking the car. All I wanted to do was to go home and have a hot bath and an early night. As we arrived at the theatre, it was hot, crowded and noisy. Inwardly I groaned and gritted my teeth as we pushed our way through the crowds to try to find a place to stand. Within about 5 or 10 minutes I became energised and much more positive about the evening in front of me. The concert had not started but what I had picked up on was the collective anticipation of the audience or "positive vibes". I had fed off of that energy and become uplifted.

Synchronicity is another facet of spiritual development which should not be discounted. Synchronicity or coincidence such as when you have a telephone call from someone you have just been thinking about for example can be an illustration of your intuitive abilities starting to develop.

Synchronicity was a concept which Carl Jung, a psychiatrist, expolored. He believed that we are all part of a "collective unconscious" suggesting that within the unconscious minds of everyone, universal keys of knowledge exist.

Becoming aware of synchronistic happenings is a good way of acknowledging on a day to day basis that there is more "guidance" within our lives than we realise.

As our spiritual development continues, dreams sometimes become more vivid and memorable. If you have a particularly clear dream it is a good idea to try to understand the sub-conscious messages which you are being given. There are many books that will provide explanations to the symbolic meanings of your dreams, but try initially to fathom out the meanings for yourself.

Some common signs within dreams can be interpreted as follows:

DEATH - this, although unsettling, can be an indication of entering into a new phase within your life. It can be symbolic of the ending of something which is outmoded.

BIRTH - could be about a boby but can also signify new beginnings.

FLYING - can indicate a need for freedom

HOUSE OR BUILDINGS - are symbolic of the self. The rooms are aspects of the self which may need to be addressed.

MOUNTAINS- can illustrate obstacles that need to be overcome or a point that you need to reach in your life.

GARDENS - are thought to be representative of the self so if you dream of a garden which is in full flower then perhaps you are blooming in an aspect of your life. If it is chaotic and untidy perhaps you need to bring more focus to aspects within you.

Some people, as part of their development keep a record of their dreams that they can revisit at later dates. There are also numerous occasions when people, famous and otherwise, have been given inspiration and answers from their dreams. If you wish to keep a dream diary, always ensure that you have a pen and paper by the bed as you tend to lose the detail of the dreams when you try to record them at a later date.

As your intuition develops begin to take notice of the signals that you receive. Try to acknowledge and honour the connections that you are being given. This process seems to aid and enhance the receptivity of this part of spiritual development. A good exercise to help the process is to try Psychometry. All you need to do is to sit quietly, holding an object such as a set of keys, or a piece of jewellery that belongs to someone else. Try to tap into the energetic information which the piece gives off by closing your eyes and becoming aware of any emotions, thoughts or reactions you get whilst holding it. If you can get feedback from another person about your responses you may be extremely surprised at the ability we all have to connect on deeper levels with inanimate objects in order to pick up the personal vibrations which can be absorbed from each and every one of us.

Meditation as well as any form of spiritual/vibrational healing and therapies, massage, reflexology, aromatherapy etc. can help us to make powerful transitions on a physical level - this is generally accepted. However, all of these tools help to work on the subtle energetic imbalances and blocks within the mental, emotional and physical too. Most therapists, whatever their therapy may be, recognise that clients can go through what is sometimes known as a "healing crisis" or "healing reaction".

The most common experiences are heightened emotional state (can be a positive or negative state), flu-like symptoms which come on quickly and go just as quickly, an awareness of and increase in dreams which seem to be more vivid, a worsening of the condition which was being treated followed by an improvement and so on.

Most therapists regard these signs as a positive indication that energy has been shifted, although it is hard to acknowledge this and feel good about it if you are on the receiving end of a healing crisis!

If you find that you are experiencing reactions to treatments or work done with any vibrational tools, try to discern how you feel and whether it seems appropriate.

The first time I was aware of a healing crisis, I experienced flu-like symptoms following a crystal healing session with someone I trusted completely. I was aware that I had been rushing around too much and this "illness" or reaction made me sit still and take stock. It gave me time to think things through, which was something that I needed to do but at that moment I would have found it difficult to give myself permission to take the time out.

A good reference book may be *Heal Your Body* by Louise Hay, which gives symptoms and details of what the symptoms could be trying to tell you by manifesting. It also gives positive affirmations to help the process along. In this book for example Louise Hay suggests that coughs can be a physical manifestation of an indication that the sufferer "desires to bark at the world". "See me, Listen to me" and that Constipation indicates an unwillingness to "release old ideas. Stuck in the past. Sometimes stinginess"!

Personally, I feel that the suggestions in her book should be considered and adapted, as the individual feels necessary.

Every person is different and I would suggest that there are many reasons that illnesses manifest and those suggestions in this book may have great relevance for some but no relevance for others. It can also be extremely detrimental for anyone to tell another that the illness they are suffering from is their own creation and that they are to blame for their own suffering if they not in the correct frame of mind to accept this information. It may also be that there are other more complicated reason such as karma or lessons being learned or past life history which is being reflected in this lifetime (for example, those who believe in reincarnation accept that it is possible to "hold onto" an injury from a past life by incarnating with an illness which is explained when they have explored a trauma which occurred in a past life)

Whatever the cause of the illness, affirmations are a powerful yet simple way of working with the mind in order to bring about positive changes and healing effects. Affirmations can be incorporated into meditation routines by following these simple guidelines:-

i) They should always be in the present tense

II) They should always be phrased in a positive way

Notice what happens if you are asked not to think of something - it becomes difficult to wipe that thought out. If you tell a child that they will spill the drink in their cup then this immediately becomes a possibility in the child's mind and the focus is placed upon the negative rather than the positive. If we use self limiting language we are reinforcing the negative beliefs or behavioural patterns which we wish to change. Try to become aware of the amount of times that you say negative things about yourself to others, such as "I am so shy" or "I am fat" and replace them with more positive statements. If you find that these negative comments fly out of your mouth before you can stop them, change them into a positive statement immediately.

Examples of affirmations could be "I like my body", "I am loveable", "I enjoy meeting others and they enjoy meeting me", "I am living in the NOW".

I feel that affirmations have greater power if you construct them yourself and if when repeating the affirmation you incorporate a visualisation of yourself which has relevance to the changes you wish to bring about, you will find that the whole process becomes doubly empowered. For example, if you are affirming that you are confident and extrovert, mentally create a picture of yourself as an assured and outgoing member of a group.

Affirmations and positive visualisations can be used during meditation, any time during the day when you can "daydream", such as when you are on a train or a bus, when you are about to fall asleep etc. You can simply mentally or verbally say them over and over again or possibly create a recording which you can easily listen to.

Opening your mind up to all these possibilities can take quite a leap of faith. Try not to rush the process, as this is usually counter-productive. Simply affirm that you will keep an open mind and take time to honour, acknowledge and understand the experiences which you have. Some people find that their progress is slower than others. This is not necessarily an indication that someone is more or less spiritual, worthy, aware or so on than you, so try not to judge yourself or others. Each person develops in a unique way which is both personal and appropriate to him or her. Sometimes things move at a rapid pace and other times things move at a slower pace when these experiences are consolidated and refined.

Try not to get frustrated and give up. Going with the flow and living in the moment is an important lesson which we all have to learn. You are entering a path which will be exciting, frustrating, powerful, sometimes frightening but which will lead to greater self awareness and a deeper understanding of the natural energies which we can access for healing ourselves, others and the world as well as both spiritual and personal development.

2. Learning to Dowse

Almost everyone can dowse. As with most things there are people to whom this ability comes naturally and others who find it a little more difficult. In most cases all that is required is a little open-mindedness and some perseverance.

The two most common instruments used for dowsing are rods and pendulums - see DIAGRAM 2 Rods and pendulums

You can buy pendulums made from crystals, brass, glass etc. or you can simply make one yourself by suspending a cork, button, or a piece of jewellery such as a ring on a piece of string or a chain.

In terms of ease of use and portability most people opt for pendulums but certainly when working with earth energies for example people tend to prefer working with rods.

Rods can be simply made by cutting two wire coat hangers and bending to shape. See DIAGRAM 3 - Coat Hangers

When using rods you simply hold one in each hand and walk towards the area where you are trying to locate water, energy lines etc. A good way to practice this ability is to hide a coin under a rug. Walk towards the rug with the intent that the rods will indicate where the coin is placed. You may find that the rods will change position depending on how you hold them. It is important to note that everyone has their own individual reactions which indicate positive, negative and

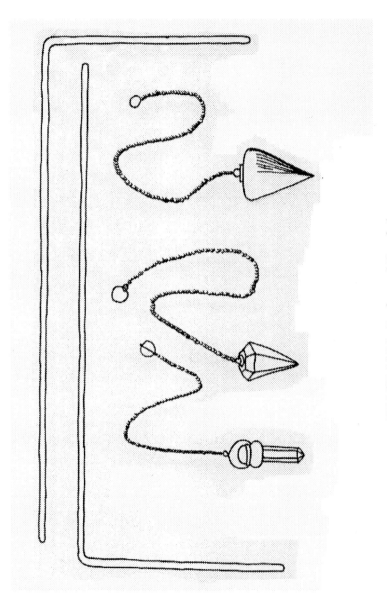

DIAGRAM 2 - Rods and Pendulums

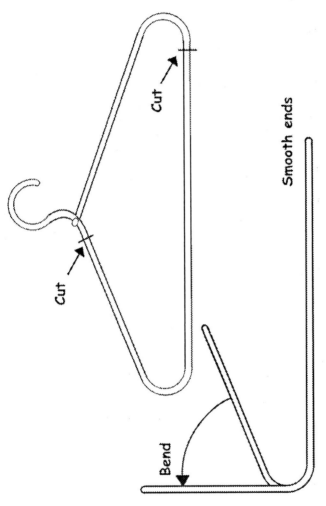

Cut

Cut

Smooth ends

Bend

EASY TO MAKE DOWSING ROD

DIAGRAM 3 - Coat Hangers

19

neutral. By practicing you will be able to ascertain what your indications are for these.

The reactions obtained by an instrument when dowsing, have been very difficult for science to explain, but the most popular theory which has been put forward and, to some extent, accepted is that the pendulum or rod amplifies the brain rhythms and muscular responses in order to show the answer via the pendulum or rod. Other ideas such as the answer being obtained by Earth energies combining with the personal energies belonging to the person dowsing have been suggested, but so far nothing has been substantiated.

To the lay person, dowsing is associated perhaps with the old timer who finds water by divining with a forked stick, although dowsing is still commonly used today for things as widespread as medical diagnosis, healing, agricultural uses i.e., soil testing, site surveying, mineral prospecting, tracing lost objects and so on.

Experienced dowsers can use it for a variety of personal reasons such as where to place furniture such as beds, how to find lost objects, or even where to go on holiday by dowsing over a map.

For the purposes of this book, it is an invaluable tool to enable us to 'see' energy and measure its strength or weakness.

When dowsing it is important to understand that your positive and negative signs are individual to you and that there is no right or wrong ways as was illustrated when using the rod. When working with the pendulum, the "yes" and "no" answers may be shown by the pendulum moving in a clock-wise, anti-clockwise, up, down or diagonal direction. Only practising through trial and error will show you what is correct for you.

The first thing that you should do is to make yourself comfortable and relaxed. Try not to attach any emotions to what you are about to do or to the outcome, as this can affect your ability to dowse and the result.

Hold the pendulum with your thumb and forefinger pointing down. If you wish to rest your elbow on a table, then do so. Keep the chain or thread of the pendulum reasonably short, about 5-7cm as the shorter this is, the quicker the pendulum will respond.

Begin by asking the pendulum either verbally or mentally to show you your yes. Repeat the question over and over again until it starts to move. Once you have been shown the answer from the pendulum, ask it other questions to which you know the answer will be yes.

When you are happy with the yes response, start the process again but this time asking to be shown the no response. The pendulum may move in the opposite direction to your yes or it may move in a different way. Repeat the process as with the yes response by asking questions to which you expect to get a no response.

Over a period of about a week or two, keep doing these exercises, gradually interspersing them with questions you do not know the answer to. This will help you gain confidence and trust in what you are doing. It will also make you quicker and more proficient.

Once you are more confident, you can practice with the skill by asking questions of the pendulum which will help you to locate something that has been hidden by someone else, water pipes, etc., or even simply tossing a coin and dowsing to see if it is heads or tails before looking at the coin. It is generally considered that on average, effective dowsers can achieve a success rate of about 70%.

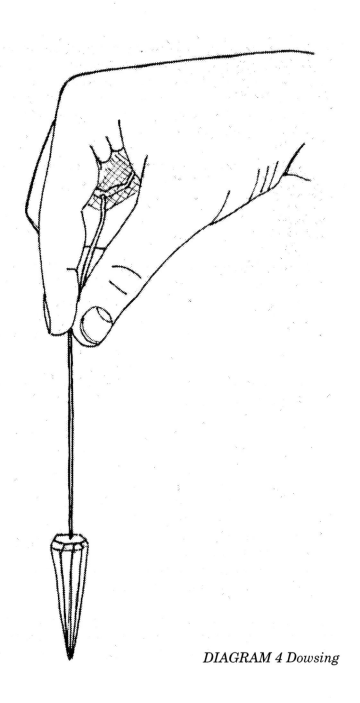

DIAGRAM 4 Dowsing

Another good exercise is to dowse a crystal for energy. All crystals emit a piezoelectric charge and if you hold a pendulum over a crystal, it invariably moves in a positive direction so long as the crystal is in a healthy state, i.e. cleansed and positively charged. (For more information on this - refer to Chapter 5)

When dowsing, it is important to remember the following rules:

> Never dowse for gain i.e. the lottery numbers, it never works.

> Never dowse for the answer to something that you either wish to happen or think you know. You are working with the subconscious and if you are not detached from the result, the conscious can have an effect on the outcome of the answer, which may, ultimately, give you the wrong conclusion.

> Always ask permission to dowse when dowsing on behalf of someone else.

> When dowsing always ensure that your energy field is protected from outside negative forces.

> Always be aware of how you phrase your questions, it is surprising how the answer can be altered by inaccurate phrasing. For example, do not ask if you have lost something you are looking for as the answer will obviously be Yes! Instead ask if it is possible for you to find the object and then proceed from there to possible locations where it may be found.

As you progress with dowsing you may feel that you would like more refinement of the questions you ask so I have included a couple of charts which serve as examples as to the

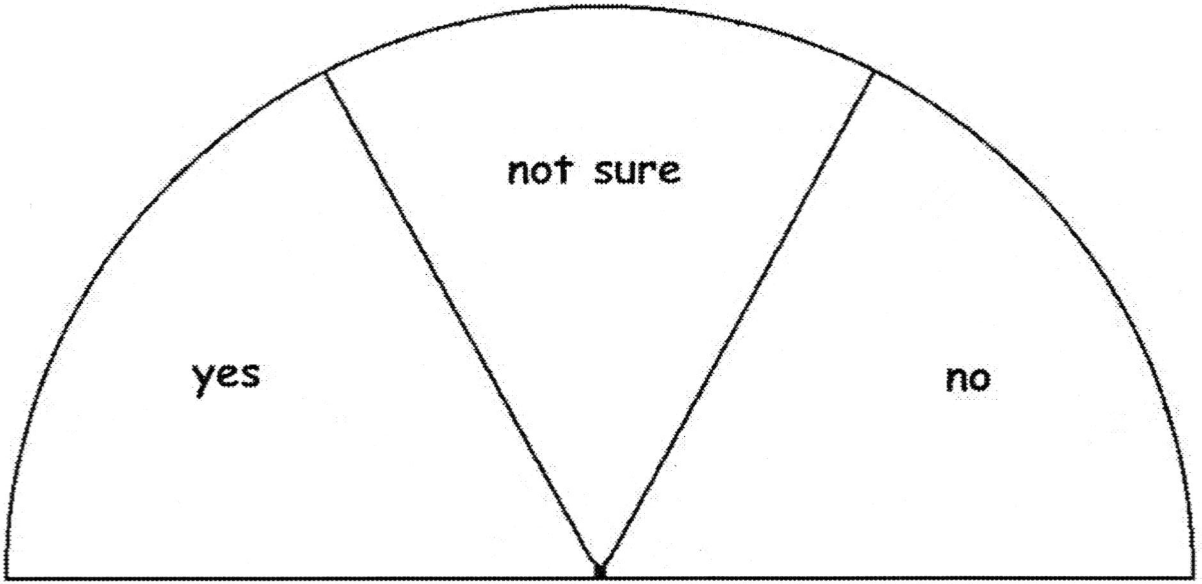

DIAGRAM 5 - YES / NO / MAYBE CHART

yes

not sure

no

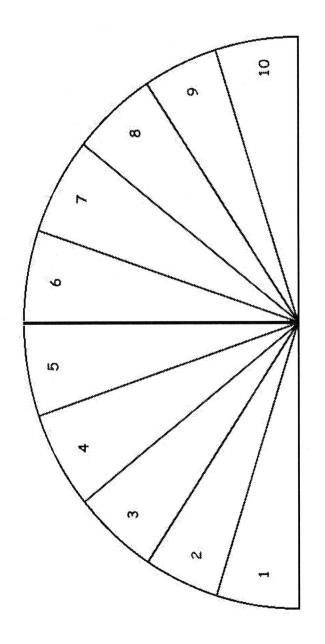

DIAGRAM 6 - NUMBER CHART

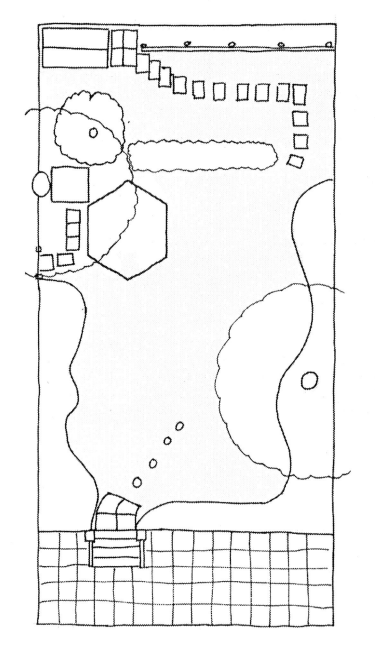

DIAGRAM 7 Locating hidden items (3)

kind of aids which you can create to help you gather more information from your pendulum.

The uses that dowsing can be put to are endless and are subject to only the restrictions of your own creativity. Here are a few suggestions to get you started:

Dowsing for food intolerance and allergies

Dowsing for flower remedies

Dowsing to select a crystal

Dowsing to see if a crystal needs to be cleansed or charged.

Dowsing sacred sites and maps.

Dowsing chakras - see next chapter.

At the end of the day, dowsing is a tool with which you can develop your intuition. It is a skill, which is easily learned with a little application and patience and which when used with integrity, and grace will reward you with a valued tool to aid your spiritual growth and physical wellbeing.

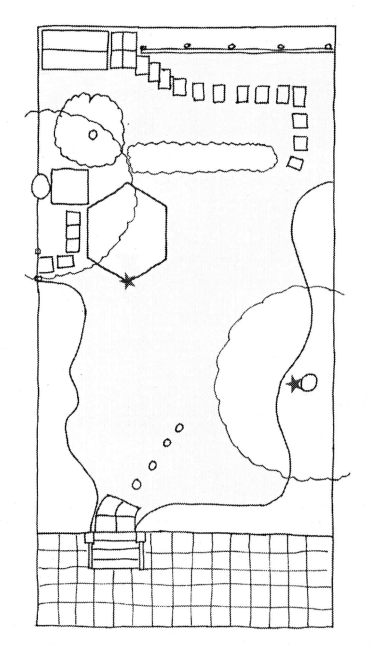

DIAGRAM 8 Locating hidden items (2)

3. Human Energy - Accessing and Working with the Chakra, Meridian and Auric Systems of the Body

The energetic systems of the body are hard to see but easier to feel. A good exercise to begin with is to rub the palms of your hands together and then hold them with the palms facing towards each other but with the distance of about 10-12 inches or 25-30 cms between the hands. Then start to 'bounce'î your hands together, becoming aware of either a feeling of resistance (a bit like when you put magnets together the wrong way and they repel instead of connect), heat, draught, and pressure.

Everybody feels the energy in different ways so experiment with what you are feeling. It sometimes helps to close your eyes to aid concentration. Practice with this until you are sure of what you are sensing. When you begin to feel the energy stop, rest your arms and hands, and then reconnect. As you become more confident with what you are feeling, you will find that you will be able to connect with the energy more quickly.

Although the body is generally regarded in the western world as composed of purely the physical, many eastern religion and medical practices recognise an energetic presence within the body. They believe that if attention is paid to the energetic imbalances, which occur when the body is under mental, emotional, physical or even spiritual distress, then steps can be taken in order to prevent illness manifesting into the physical parts of the body.

Chakras

Many of the eastern-based religions are one step ahead of us in recognising and working with the Chakra Systems in the body.

It is believed that these centres take in and give out prana, chi or life force energy. They are also considered to be major intersections (i.e. roundabouts) linking in with Meridians and minor chakra points.

In order for the person to be in good health, it is important that these centres remain aligned, energised and balanced. When the balance is thrown out, the body becomes stressed and this in turn can bring about a state of ill health. Any number of factors can put the body into this state of dis-ease and these factors can be related to mental, physical, emotional or spiritual imbalances.

Today, even the medical profession accepts that the onset of some illnesses can be traced back to stressful or traumatic situations that the patient has been subject to and many physical illnesses are now commonly accepted as being stress related such as blood pressure, heart problems, skin disorders, digestive disorders and so on to name just a few.

Although it is commonly accepted that we have hundreds of minor Chakra points on the body, there are 7 major Chakras. These centres are perceived by Clairvoyants as being cone shaped and protruding out of the body. In the case of the

Brow, Throat, Heart, Solar Plexus and Sacral, they stick out both front and back. The Base and Crown Chakras only focus downwards and upwards respectively. Clairvoyants are people who have the gift or knack of being able to see the energetic body and some can identify imbalances by "reading" the colours which are reflected in the chakras and the energy field surrounding the body. SEE DIAGRAM 9 - Aura

Each centre is perceived as having a colour vibration and an aspect of the physical, mental and spiritual body combined to which it relates.

The major 7 are as follows:-

Crown Chakra - This Chakra is based on the Crown of the head. Its colour is usually seen as Violet or Purple but some people find it easier to visualise as pure White.

The Crown Chakra is believed to be the nearest connection between the spiritual aspect of the person and God.

It is commonly accepted to be the centre, which receives intuition whether it is from God, Angels Guides or as some believe the subconscious. On a physical level, the Crown relates to the Pineal gland and covers the upper brain and right eye areas of the body.

Third Eye Chakra is located just slightly above and between the eyebrows. The colour indigo is allied to this centre

The Third Eye or Brow Chakra relates to the intuitive ability of the person. It is linked to psychic abilities and power. When functioning clearly, the Brow Chakra enables one to receive higher guidance. In addition to this, this centre allows one to focus on purifying negative thoughts and behavior patterns.

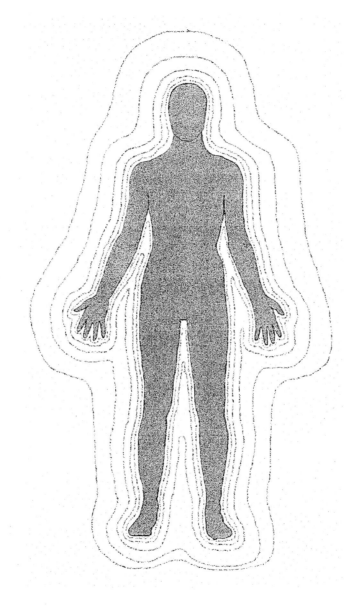

DIAGRAM 9 - Aura

Physically, the Third Eye Chakra is linked to the lower brain, left eye, ears, nose and nervous system as well as the Pituitary gland.

The Throat Chakra is found at the neck, in the centre just above the collarbone. Its colour is light blue.

The Throat Chakra is the centre concerned with communication of all kinds such as creativity, art, writing, music etc. as well as the ability to understand and to make oneself understood by others.

The Throat Chakra covers the Thyroid gland, Bronchial and vocal mechanics of the body, Lungs and Alimentary Canal.

The Heart Chakra is in the centre of the chest but at the level of the physical heart. Colour for this centre is traditionally light green but some people prefer to work with light pink at this centre.

The Heart Chakra relates to the ability to love oneself and others, ideally unconditionally.

Physically linked to the Thymus gland, Heart, Blood, Vagus nerve, Circulatory system.

The Solar Plexus Chakra is found in the solar plexus area which is just above the bellybutton in most cases. The colour yellow is linked to this centre.

The Solar Plexus Chakra is the seat of the emotions. Who has not felt ìbutterflies in their stomachî, ìa sinking feeling in the pit of the stomachî etc. It is believed that this centre is responsible for ambition, personal power, and intellect.

In addition to this, it is thought by some to be the 'energetic mouth' of the body where prana, chi or life force energy is

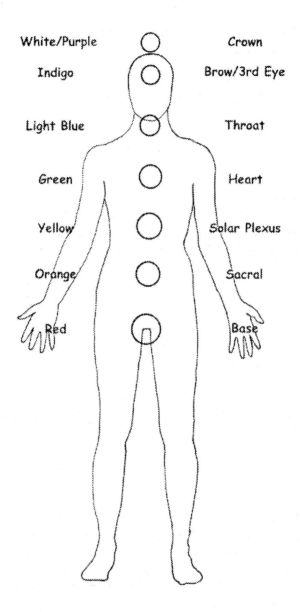

White/Purple	Crown
Indigo	Brow/3rd Eye
Light Blue	Throat
Green	Heart
Yellow	Solar Plexus
Orange	Sacral
Red	Base

DIAGRAM 10 - The Chakras

drawn in before being spread throughout the body via the meridian system.

The Solar Plexus Chakra covers the Pancreas, Stomach, Liver, Gall Bladder and Nervous System.

The Sacral Chakra is based usually about 2 or 3 inches below the belly button and linked to the colour orange.

The Sacral Chakra is the centre linked to the reproductive and sexual functions as well as possibly being the centre which governs the well-being of the physical and thereby, it is this centre which allows conditions to arise in the body to highlight 'dis-ease'. Once the dis-ease is addressed, this will hopefully bring about a realignment of the mind, body and spirit. This then allows every part of the body to function at its optimum level. Physically linked to the Gonads and Reproductive System.

The Base Chakra is located at the base of the spine, in the lumbar region. Red is the colour related to this centre.

The Base Chakra is linked to survival on the physical plane as opposed to spiritual. Someone suffering from depression might find that his or her Base Chakra was very weak for example. It is the centre linked with vitality and the will. This centre governs over the physical aspects of the Adrenal glands, Spinal Column and Kidneys.

Many healers start with working on the Chakras to clear, rebalance and realign them, by channeling energy which they receive after linking to God or a higher source. In some instances they may be 'inspired' to concentrate on one particular centre which is out of balance or simply top up the energy of each centre.

When the chakras become blocked the chi energy or prana flow is inhibited. Here is a suggested list of possible symptoms of chakra imbalances:

Base - Feelings of unworthiness, not being understood, not loved. May possibly be an indication of someone who is too materialistic, wanting more because of lack of security in the past. The person may be dominant with an intense survival instinct (possibly as a result of not being looked after as a child). These feelings can stem from this or past lives. If this centre is out of balance the person may not want to be "here". On a physical level, they may have problems with legs, hips, coccyx.

Sacral - Great difficulty in trusting, fear of being left alone but fear of loving. Imbalances in sexual contact i.e. frigid or promiscuous, sexual dependency. Fear of having a relationship, wanting it too much, tendency to be tense about sexuality, instability, and addictions to anything from love to drugs - abuse or misuse. Physically, they may have problems in the area of the large intestine.

Solar Plexus - May be indicated by someone who is helpless and weak. Allowing themselves to be controlled. Someone who has no natural ability to balance control and dominance. Shows off and struggles for success. Can hold suppressed anger and possibly suddenly expresses this through anger or rage. Misuse of power, aggressive, enjoying arguments. Passive power through helplessness. Physically it may manifest as digestive problems, migraine, weaknesses with the immune system.

Heart Chakra - Loneliness, lost, not enough attention, sad without a reason, guilt. Possible origins not enough love when we are little.

Tendency to exaggerate or to set aside own desires for others. Plays the role of victim. Constant search for new relationships. The person may be depressed, repressed having a fear of being their own self. Physically it could surface as Asthma, air-based allergies such as hay-fever etc.

Throat Chakra - Unable to express themselves through singing talking , movement. Criticism, punishment whilst speaking own truth could be the origins of the block. Feelings of not being good enough, not being understood. Can be blocked with unexpressed grief. Men can be more prone towards getting blockages in this area as blockages may be caused by unexpressed emotions. Blockages in this area may manifest in the person having a tendency to manipulate or lie. Lack of clarity and inability to make up their minds about things although this can also be a symptom of blocks within the Solar Plexus. Manifests physically as thyroid difficulties, neck problems.

3rd Eye Chakra - Very criticising, very judgmental. Not happy or convinced, nothing is good enough. Great difficulty - experiences periods of time when intuition and logic struggles with each other. Unable to see links or patterns in things, not wanting to look beyond the obvious.

Crown Chakra - Disturbed connection with the Divine and or universal energy, this centre is rarely blocked but more often out of balance. It can manifest as delusion, illusion and by the person being only interested in "spiritual" or "wordly" things- can't deal with both. Physically can manifest as Dyslexia, Dyspraxia, general co-ordination.

SEE DIAGRAM 11 - Chakra imbalances

In order to clear these blockages/imbalances, it is important to:

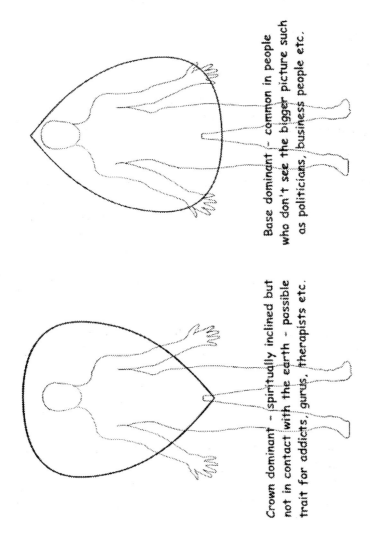

Crown dominant – spiritually inclined but not in contact with the earth – possible trait for addicts, gurus, therapists etc.

Base dominant – common in people who don't see the bigger picture such as politicians, business people etc.

DIAGRAM 11 - Chakra Imbalances

Understand why WE have allowed them to be created in the first place.

Not to project guilt and blame onto others for example parents or partners

Try to see what it has taught us.

Ask have I learned my lesson?

Forgive - especially oneself.

Usually, the Base and Heart chakras work as a pair as do the Throat and Sacral and the Solar Plexus and Crown/Brow. This means that there can be imbalances or conflicts between these centres.

Try to become conscious of negative thoughts and emotions. Know that it is possible to release them through understanding of the greater truth. Try to work from a position of unconditional love and compassion for us and others.

You can become aware of these centres by using the following methods:

Dowsing with a pendulum. By holding the pendulum over the Chakra centres you should be able to see the pendulum swirl in an alternate clockwise/anti clockwise motion as you move down each chakra. This method also allows you to become aware of how balanced each chakra is in relation to the others.

By standing at the side of your 'patient' slowly draw your hands down their back and front. As you come to the location of the chakra you should be able to feel the energy of each centre. Most people feel a pressure, tingling, heat or cold on these 'hotspots' of energy.

Note carefully if the centres are balanced. It is necessary to understand that the chakras can be over energised as well as under energised, so use your discernment and intuition to decide. Take into account what is happening to the person on a physical, mental, emotional or even spiritual level.

Over energised chakras may not necessarily indicate good health but may indicate an inability to "hold" the energy in the body having the effect of a leaking bucket. People with over energised centres may find that they lack energy and are listless and lethargic. Whilst for some with what appears to be under energised centres you may discern that they are hyperactive and prone to overdoing things.

As humanity progresses, many people are becoming aware that the chakra system is changing and a new set of chakras are beginning to infiltrate the energy systems of highly spiritually evolved people. They are seen clairvoyantly as different colours to the original and usually start to become connected to the energy system as people move from the 3rd dimension into the 4th. In other words, they become connected equally to the spiritual as well as the physical in the 4th dimension as opposed to living purely in the physical.

Opinions vary as to the combination of colours but below I offer some suggestions taken from a book by Diana Cooper called "*A Little Light On Ascension*" . Another version of the new colours for chakras may be obtained from "*The Healing Book*" by Chris Thomas and Diane Baker. My personal feeling is that as we develop and shift we become more in tune with what feels right and what feels wrong. This is discernment of our own individual truth and a process which is important in that we need to become aware of our own truths in order that we have no longer need of Gurus, leaders and religions and so on. We become our own Master. Therefore it follows that if you have reached a point where the "new" chakras are becoming activated, you will be more aware of your truth and thereby be enabled to work with the colours which are the most appropriate to you.

The following is a list from "*A Little Light On Ascension*":

Base - Pearl White: as this chakra becomes part of our system we begin to function from a position of joy and delight instead of survival.

Sacral - Luminous Pink-Orange: indicates an equal balance of the masculine and feminine energies within the whole.

Solar Plexus - Gold: indicating a higher wisdom, confidence and power allowing us to feel centered and focussed without fear whatever the circumstances.

Heart - pale violet pink: signifying unconditional love.

Throat - blue violet colour: opening us up more fully to psychic gifts and healing abilities.

3rd Eye - Translucent golden white: opening us up to thoughts of a higher and purer vibration and higher levels of clairvoyance and prophecy.

Crown Chakra - White violet: allowing for us to connect more fully with the Higher Self or Soul.

These colours are taken from *The Healing Book* by Chris Thomas and Diane Baker In this book they use more than one colour for the chakras and as they point out in the book the colours are:-

Root Chakra main colour coppery gold, with 'fins' of violet, gold and blue.
Second chakra main colour blue, with 'fins' of violet, gold and coppery-gold
Third Chakra main colour an equal mixture of blue and gold, with 'fins' of violet, gold and blue
Fourth Chakra main colour silver with flecks of gold, with

'fins' of random mixtures of violet, green, blue and coppery-gold.

Fifth Chakra and above are basically the same with swirling patterns of gold, blue and violet on a transparent background. As you go up the chakras towards the crown the number of flecks reduces until you arrive at the crown which is totally transparent.

If these colours feel more appropriate than the initial colours outlined at the beginning of the chapter, simply substitute them in the meditation.

The Auric Field

Most people believe there to be 7 layers composing the Auric Field or Aura. These 7 layers are associated with the 7 main chakras as listed above, thus the layer nearest to the body is linked to the base chakra, the next layer which is generated by the sacral chakra, is projected around the body after the first.

These layers flow, expand and contract as the person experiences various stimuli via the mental, physical, spiritual and emotional.

The field can be felt and as one develops their ability to feel energy fields it is possible to become sensitive enough to feel the layers as you pass your hands through them.

Some people are able to 'see' the aura around a person's body and there are even therapists who are able to detect imbalances within the auric field. If you wish to explore the possibility of seeing the aura, the following exercise is a good one to try.

Light a candle and place the candle in front of you at eye level.

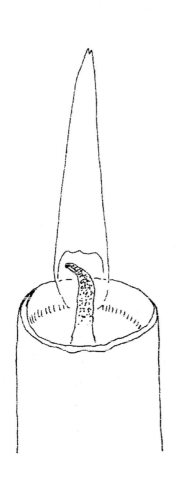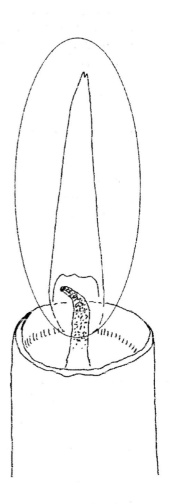

DIAGRAM 12

It is preferable to have the candle standing in front of a dark background. Begin by staring at the candle flame. As you stare at the flame you will become aware of the feint hazy aura that surrounds the actual flame. When you can see this focus on it and you will see that the aura starts to expand out even further.

You may even begin to detect colours within the milky aura.

The aura around the body can be perceived in much the same way and usually the first thing that can be seen is a milky kind of haze especially around the head. It can help to allow the eyes not to focus directly onto the person or object whose aura they are trying to see but to gaze in an indistinct way as one would when one is lost in thought and sitting at a window or attempting to see a 'magic eye' picture.

When trying to see a person's aura it is usually best to get them to sit in front of a plain background but play around with different backgrounds and see what works for you. When I have been teaching there have been quite marked differences in the perceptions of my pupils. Some can pick up on the colours straight away, but for the majority it seems to be something that they have to work at developing. If you can do this with a group of friends, it is best to have one person sitting alone whilst the others try to focus and share what they are seeing. This way each member of the group is providing 'proof' to the others.

Within the body there are 12 main Meridian systems which are divided into 6 Yin and 6 Yang. Yin and Yang relates to balance and harmony, that is the basis of health. They are opposing forces that are linked and need to be maintained in perfect balance for good health. The Yin sign is seen as feminine, passive, cold, negative, dark. The Yang sign is viewed as masculine, warm, light, positive, active.

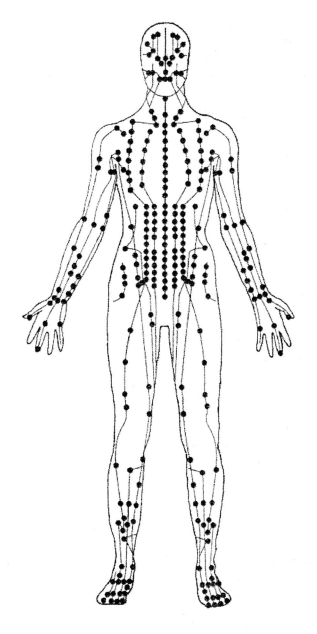

DIAGRAM 13 - Meridian System

The Meridian systems channel energy throughout the body and each one is linked to an organ or function such as the Liver or Heart. Throughout the Meridians there are 365 main acupuncture points. If the energy flows freely and unhindered the body remains healthy but if it should become blocked, out of balance or sluggish, there may be adverse physical reactions to this 'dis-ease' which could result in a reaction within the physical, mental or emotional well-being of that person.

Acupuncturists work on these lines to free up the energy and allow it to flow unimpeded in a balanced and healthy way in order to bring about optimum opportunities for the body to regain its own equilibrium. Although it is commonly accepted that Acupuncturists use needles to unblock the energy, there is a growing band of therapists trained to work with Crystals in order to realign the flow of chi, prana or life-force energy.

As we begin to understand that there is more to ourselves than just the physical body, it becomes apparent that purely taking medication alone for example, may not be the optimum way of addressing disease within the body. It follows, therefore that it may be appropriate to also consider relevant therapies, which will help to address the energetic implications of the physical breakdown. Self help techniques are simply to visualise the flow of energy in meditation as increasing. It could possibly help to hold a clear quartz point or termination in the left and right hand with one termination pointing up and one down. Then visualise the energy flowing from the crystal pointing up going into the body, flushing through the meridian, clearing any blocks, whilst the other crystal which is pointing downwards, simply draws out the old energy. As soon as you feel that the energy is cleared finish the meditation but ensure that both crystals are thoroughly cleansed afterwards. (See chapter 5).

Cross Crawl Exercise To Increase And Balance The Flow Of Energy

Stand up straight, ensuring that you have enough room to swing your arms without coming into contact with anything or anyone.

Then, raise your right arm at the same time as raising your left leg and bring down your right arm so that it touches the left knee. Return arm and leg and repeat the process using this time the left arm and the right leg. Do this exercise several times. It is particularly effective for people who are dyslexic as it helps them to think more clearly, improve co-ordination and balance by harmonizing the energies within the left and right hemispheres of the brain.

Another quick way to focus before writing or studying for example is to simply draw a figure of eight sideways going over the figure several times. This has the same effect as above in correcting the balance between the left and right hemisphere of the brain.

The Importance of Protecting the Energy Field

The energy field of the body is extremely susceptible to outside influences. Who, for instance, hasn't felt drained when speaking to someone who is in a negative frame of mind, even over the telephone, or uplifted after having spoken to someone who is in an upbeat, joyful mood.

Taken on a larger scale, try to remember the uncomfortable atmosphere in an audience when, for instance a comedian is not making them laugh or the energy generated by the crowd as a footballer attempts to score a goal from the penalty box and their reaction when he either succeeds or fails.

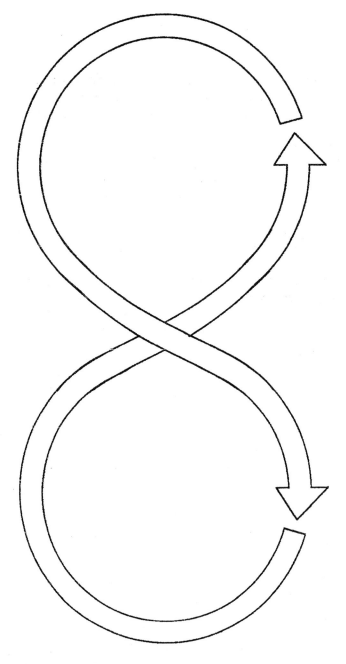

DIAGRAM 14 - Figure of 8

Many people are aware of the undercurrents that go on in ordinary everyday social situations, where we cover up our true reactions to what people say and do to us in order to be polite.

This is a form of psychic awareness, which is often disregarded by us because it is so 'normal'. It could be argued that this is one of the reasons that our ability to connect with all forms of psychic ability such as intuition, telepathy, psychometry and so is now no longer inborne in most people and has to be relearned or reactivated.

It is apparent that within a circle of people of more than average highly developed psychic awareness, the undercurrents that go on through social interaction are much more complicated due to the extreme sensitivity that is engendered by these people which is not always conducive to a heightened atmosphere of love and light and is also proof that psychic ability does not automatically denote spirituality within the person.

On a individual, day to day level, we are living in a world where it is almost inevitable that we will have some kind of social connection with others. Our energy field can be affected in a positive or negative way, to a greater or lesser degree by each encounter whether it be standing next to someone on the train without a word passing anyone's lips, speaking to a friend or relation or simply thinking about someone.

Advocates of Feng Shui and space clearing also believe that our energy field can be affected by the life force within a building and by discarnate entities for example.

To safeguard our energetic health from these outside influences, there are many simple and effective ways, which fall into 2 categories:

Prevention of Damage to the Energy Body

Visualizing yourself in an egg or bubble of light, which surrounds the auric field allowing in positive energy but blocking out everything else. You can be creative with the egg or bubble using different colours to bring in added protection where you feel necessary for example. This is a good visualisation to use at the end of a meditation

Wear or carry a protective crystal. A good choice of crystal may be Carnelian which is grounding and protective or Amethyst which is a general protector however there is a multitude of choice with crystals and generally if you look at a display with the intent that you be shown the crystal which is right for you, your eye will be drawn to an appropriate crystal. See yourself in a circle of violet flame, which surrounds and protects you .

Imagine yourself covered in a protective cloak which has a hood which goes over your head, is full length and wraps around you so that not even your hands are visible.

Repair of Damage to the Energy Body

Cleansing the aura by visualising a spiral of energy swirling through the aura, a bit like a tornado, taking away any negative attachments and drawing them into the earth where they are transmuted and changed into positive energy.

Bathing in Bicarbonate of Soda is said to be cleansing for the auric field. This process can be even more effective if you use essential oils such as Basil, Frankincense, Rosemary or Spikenard as well.

Using two cleansed quartz crystals, preferably points or terminations. Place them in each hand and if using points ensure that the point on the left hand is directed towards the

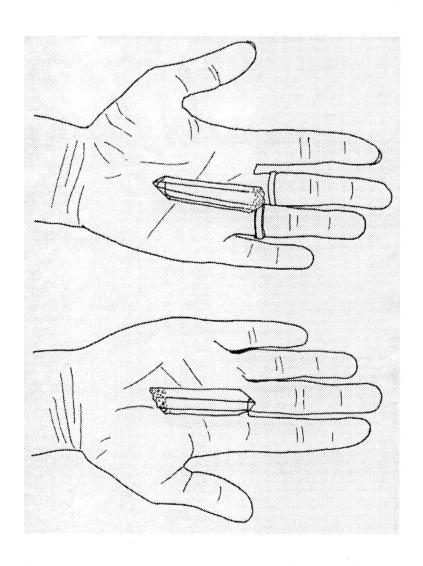

DIAGRAM 15 - Hands with crystals

body and the point in the right hand is directed away from the body. Breathe very deeply, sighing out 3 times to aid grounding. Try to still the mind and when you feel ready, connect with the crystal that you are holding in the LEFT hand. Visualise or feel the energy drawing up into the left arm and allow it to flow into the aura until it becomes full of crystal energy. See it magnetize the negative attachments to the aura and when you are ready, allow the crystal in your RIGHT hand to become activated and 'draw' the old energy out of the body and into the crystal at the same time as the crystal in your left hand is replenishing the body's energy.

When you are finished bring your focus back into the room and ensure that both crystals are thoroughly cleansed.

Working with a friend, you can test the effectiveness of the exercises above. If one of you sits comfortably on a chair whilst the other (the 'healer') stands beside the chair.

Holding your hands outstretched, the healer should centre themselves and try to sense the aura. What they may feel is a slight breeze, coolness, warmth, or a feeling of resistance against the palms of the hand. Just play with what you are feeling, relaxing your arms and then going back to reconnect with the energy until you are sure of what you are feeling. The sense of energy is very subtle but for this exercise, it is important to be sure of what you are feeling.

Once you are confident that you are aware of the feeling of the aura (if your 'patient' is sensitive, you may well find that they are conscious of your presence upon the aura), step back and allow your 'patient' to work with any of the Prevention or Repairing techniques above.

After a few moments, step closer to your 'patient' and try again to sense changes in their auric field. You will be surprised at how different techniques vary in their influence on the aura. Some will make the aura feel stronger, others will make it more difficult for you to sense the aura, whilst others will appear to contract the aura.

If the person is particularly sensitive to the energy they may well be able to detect layers by sensing areas of denseness and lightness as they pass their hands through the auric field.

Many clairvoyants who have the ability to 'see' the auras of others maintain that they can see in people's auric field, cords which have attached themselves to various chakras linking them to others. In some cases, such as those between a mother and her child these are positive and indeed necessary connections.

In other cases perhaps for example where someone is in a violent sexual relationship or even where the mother and child tie is outdated and the child has grown and needs to establish themselves as an adult, these ties are extremely negative and debilitating. When releasing from these ties, it does not mean that there will be no further contact with the person or situation, but merely bring about a shift or alteration in the dynamics of the relationship.

In dealing with the stronger ties that bind you, it may be necessary to receive extra help and support from a healer or counsellor who can aid you in detaching. However the following visualisation can be used to good effect.

Prepare the room and light a candle to draw down the light. Have a cleansing incense or essential oil burning such as Benzoin or Cypress for example. Ensure that you will not be interrupted and find a place to sit or lie where you are comfortable and relaxed.

Breathe in three times and sigh out which will help to anchor your energy. Try to still the thoughts which float through

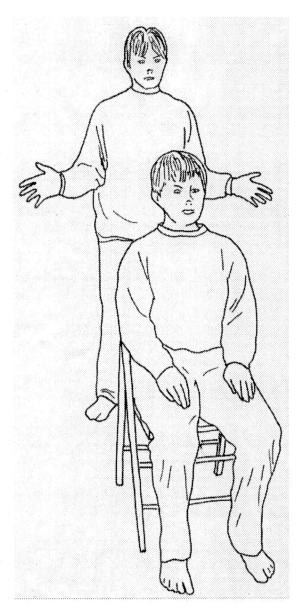

DIAGRAM 16 - Aura Sensing

your mind by seeing them as clouds in a clear blue sky which float in and out of your consciousness.

Think about the person or situation that you wish to release and try to be aware of which chakra centre or centres are affected.

Try to become aware of the strength of the connection and how it affects you and the other person. As you sense the connection, ask that if it is appropriate for the highest good of all and to the harm of none you be allowed to release this link.

When you are ready, visualize the tie being broken. Some people can do this gently by sending a pink light to release the tie whilst others feel that they need to use more drastic measures such as swords or fire in order to effect the release. Go with whatever feels right for you.

As the tie is released see it returned to the person or situation and then imagine a beam of light filling the void that has been left by the removal of the tie. Place a shield of violet light or energy or visualise a giant crystal being placed over the centres of both of you in order that the tie cannot be re-established.

Surround both of you with love, in blue and pink light. In some cases it may be necessary to repeat this a few times in order for the ties to be completely cut.

Following this exercise you should find that there is a shift or change in the relationship for the better.

A final word on grounding and centering which are techniques which should be used whenever the energy body has been influenced from things like healing, positive or negative encounters with others etc.

Grounding

If we are ungrounded, we can become unfocussed, vague. A good descriptive term is 'spaced out'. Our rational judgement may be affected and it would certainly be dangerous to drive a car for example.

In terms of spiritual development, being ungrounded may allow us to attain higher connections when we meditate but it would also mean that we would be unable to communicate anything very much from the connection once we 'return'. Therefore, it is important that a balance of as above so below is achieved. This process can be helped by using crystals for grounding such as Hematite, Apache Tear, Snowflake Obsidian, Jasper etc., by using visualisation techniques at the beginning of every meditation such as seeing our feet anchored to the floor, or creating a grounding cord, attached to the Base Chakra which is connected to the rock, tree root or stream under the earth.

Some people maintain that when they have become ungrounded in meditation, they are aware of a metallic taste in their mouths. This is thought by some to be connected to a release of hormone from the pineal gland.

Centering

When a person is not properly centered, their energy is scattered and they find it extremely difficult to live in the now. They probably are inspired with many different ideas and thoughts but that they have difficulty in acting upon any of them and therefore achieve very little.

In order to centre yourself, a good exercise is to focus on the chakra system and see them connected in a straight line. Be aware of that line becoming stronger until it becomes a column of energy which is anchored to the earth and is solid.

Try to calm the mind of the thoughts which flow through it and sit for a few minutes until a sense of peace is achieved.

Again as with grounding, it is possible for crystals to be utilised to aid the process and I would suggest possibly clear quartz or amethyst. In both cases another solution would be to select an appropriate flower essence for example Oak and Rock Rose from the Bach Flower Remedy range which are easily available in health food shops.

4. Crystals - Techniques to Work With Crystal Energies, How to Incorporate Them Into Day to Day Life

Crystal Healing is a therapy, which can be traced back as far as Egyptian times, although some would even go as far back as the mythical time of Atlantis . However, what is certain is that throughout the ages, man has used crystals and gems as talismans, symbols of authority and power, (our own Royal Family use Crowns studded with crystals and gemstones for example), tools for astrologers and diviners and, in the case of Native American Shamans, for healing purposes.

Today, there is a resurgence of interest in crystals, as people start to re-discover the intrinsic healing ability that crystals hold within them.

In the fast moving lives that we live today, it is important to take time to forge a connection with crystalline energy in order to see crystals, not merely as inanimate objects but as something which contains a life force which we can tap into. I personally feel that crystal therapy is a multi layered discipline and the deeper you connect and work with crystals, the more you become empowered to achieve with them. I would therefore urge anyone who is interested in crystals to persevere even if they feel that initially nothing is happening.

Crystals can simply be used as a focus for meditation - they have many and varied inclusions which can create rainbows. Some people find that holding a crystal can be a calming and relaxing experience whilst others find that different crystal energy can invigorate and energise them.

Other ways of using them in our day to day life is to incorporate them into your home, as in the practice of Feng Shui, where their vibrations can cleanse and redirect chi energy in a positive way. A Clear Quartz cluster placed in a room will bring the qualities of balance and harmony, whilst a chunk of Rose Quartz will radiate unconditional love into the room.

Crystals can be placed under a pillow to encourage the remembrance of dreams. In Reflexology, Aromatherapy and Massage work, they can be used to enhance the patient's therapeutic experience simply by placing them under the couch for example. They can also be used to aid the grounding process after the treatment, by introducing a grounding crystal such as Hematite, Snowflake Obsidian or Red Jasper into the patient's auric field after the treatment has been concluded.

Acupuncturists and Kinesiologists are starting to work with crystal points in order to remove blocks and provide energy when they are working for example on the Meridians within the body instead of using the more traditional (and uncomfortable!) needles.

Rose Quartz or Clear Quartz can be placed by a VDU screen, T.V., mobile phone, microwave, etc to help counteract any harmful or negative radiation.

Crystals can also provide a beautiful focus in a room, as well as generating a loving energy conducive to bringing harmony into a room. I personally have several crystals, which look beautiful when lit.

Each crystal is unique but all crystals emit a piezoelectric energy, which can be accessed by dowsing the crystal with a pendulum. This is a good way to begin to dowse as invariably one can gain a response fairly quickly. Simply hold the pendulum over the selected crystal whilst maintaining the intent and focus that the pendulum shows the energy held within the crystal. The pendulum should begin to move in a circular motion which may vary according to the amount of energy the crystal holds.

Many people find that as they develop the ability to 'tune in' to the crystal, they are able to actually feel the energy which is variously described as 'tingling', 'buzzing', 'heat', 'cold' and so on. For some it is merely a sense of knowing - and at this level it is important to trust as well as discern.

The piezoelectric energy of the crystal , when used for healing, interacts with the natural energetic field of the body and brings about a realignment in much the same way as a tuning fork helps to retune an instrument by emitting a single, constant note.

Amethyst, Rose Quartz and Clear Quartz are excellent choices of crystals for the beginner. The qualities that are generally realised by people working with crystals is that Amethyst is good for aiding meditation, protection and deep spiritual healing, Rose Quartz promotes unconditional love for the self and others and Clear Quartz aids clarity of thought and magnifies energy. This is a very general perception of these crystals and as the beginner develops they may find that there are other qualities that become more apparent and individual to each person.

It is important to note that two people working with the same crystal independently may well have different perceptions of that crystal's function. Neither is wrong, it is simply that the effect of their vibration or energy, linking with the crystal produces an individual reaction in much the same way that perfumes alter in their smell according to the chemistry of the person who is wearing it, for example.

Choosing a crystal can be done simply by buying one that you feel 'drawn' to, either by it's shape, texture, colour etc. Some people believe that you should never buy a crystal but should only work with those that are given to you. Personally, I am too impatient for that and find that over the years I have been 'drawn' to far too many crystals for my friends and families to pay for!

However, if you are given a crystal, it may well be appropriate to explore fully the qualities it brings to work with you.

Once you have purchased the crystal, the next step is to cleanse the crystal. This can be done by placing the crystal in water, visualising the crystal being cleansed, passing the crystal through smoke (i.e. 'smudging') or any other method you are guided to use. Remember however, that some water-based crystals will dissolve if left in water so check when you buy the crystal if it has any special needs. If you wish, you may like to use a pendulum to check the effectiveness of any of the above techniques.

Once the crystal has been cleansed, it should be dedicated to ensure that it can only be used for positive purposes and will not be open to any negative energy. A suggested way of dedicating your crystal is to hold the crystal and ask or think silently that this crystal be used in the name of Love and Light , for the good of all and the harm of none. You should be in a quiet place and focus your attention on the dedication as you carry it out. Find words that feel right for you.

Attunement to your crystal is a little like finding the correct radio station or frequency. If you sit quietly with the crystal in your hand, you may find that you are inspired as to the purpose for the crystal or you may have been aware of that purpose when you were first given or attracted to the crystal. Try to 'go with the flow' when working with the crystal but also try to develop your own ability to tune in to the crystal rather than depending on the definitions given in all the various books which are around. These are simply the authors' own perceptions, which may or may not be appropriate to you. There is no right or wrong meaning merely different perceptions from different people.

When holding a crystal it is usually thought that the left hand is the "receiving" hand and the right hand the "giving" hand. Therefore when working with crystals either for mediation or healing, you should hold the crystal in your left hand when you are wishing to access the crystal's qualities for the self and the right hand when you are working with the crystal to send the energy to another person, situation, place etc.,

However, as with most "rules" in this book, self-empowerment is an important part of the process and it is important that if this does not resonate or feel "right" for you that you go with what does feel correct. This may mean that you prefer the reverse position, you wish to hold the crystal in both hands or merely place the crystal within the energy field. Just follow your own instincts about what is the most appropriate for you.

These two powerful visualisations following can help with the attunement process:

Visualisation 1
Sit or lie in a comfortable position, ensuring that there are no points of tension. Place the cleansed and attuned crystal in

your receiving hand. Imagine the energy flowing from the crystal up your arm and into the heart chakra. As the heart chakra begins to fill, visualise the energy flowing into the other chakras and as they fill, flowing into the meridians which carry the energy throughout the body. Become aware of how that energy feels to be held within your physical form and allow the flow of energy to continue out of the physical and into the auric field of the body until you have reached the outer edges of your aura. Sit for a few moments and try to connect with the feelings that these processes bring. Does the crystal energy feel different when it is in the heart chakra only? How did it feel when you were merely holding it into the physical? Was there a difference when you visualized it drifting into the energetic body?

Slowly visualise the process reversing, sending the energy back into the meridians, chakras, drawing the energy back into the crystal from the heart chakra, down the arm and seeing it return to the crystal in your hand.

Breathe more deeply and slowly bring your awareness back into the room and when you are ready, open your eyes.

Visualisation 2
Again holding the cleansed and dedicated crystal in your receiving hand. Sit or lie comfortably and close your eyes. Try to see, in your mind's eye the colour or shape that forms the crystal you are holding. Become aware of the temperature of the crystal, the texture of the crystal, whether it is heavy or light, whether there are any chips, inclusions, jagged edges. Is there a particular way that you should be holding the crystal? Begin to "see", in your mind's eye, the crystal in your hand increase in size, until it is big enough for you to step into. You may find that a chip or "fault" in the crystal has grown to become a doorway. If it feels appropriate, step into the crystal and find yourself in a cave or room surrounded by

crystalline energy. It may be that the room is formed entirely from walls made of the crystal. Is there anyone else there? If so, is it a Deva or Guardian of the crystal?

Just sit quietly and after a few moments step out of the crystal cave or room and observe as the crystal starts to shrink and return to it's original shape and size. Become aware of the crystal sitting gently in your hand and when you are ready bring your focus back into the room, opening your eyes.

When you are able to connect with crystals, try the same exercise with different crystals and you will be surprised at the variations each one brings to the meditation. If you have a friend who is willing to follow the same exercise, you may find it an interesting process to compare notes on the same crystals and the reactions that each of you gained.

A good practical exercise which I have used on numerous groups in order to encourage them to feel the energy, is to hold a rough chunk of Rose Quartz about five inches above the outstretched palm of another person (many Crystal Healers believe that the left hand receives energy whilst the right hand gives. This is again something that is not cast in stone and if it doesn't feel appropriate for you, go with what does). Place your other hand underneath the outstretched palm and gently and slowly move the crystal along the length and width of the hand. The person may find that if they close their eyes initially it is easier to feel the energy from the crystal. Common perceptions from people is that they feel 'tingling', 'resistance', 'heat', 'cold', 'buzzing' and so on. If you have a Clear Quartz point or termination you could try the same exercise with this and they should be able to feel a different response - usually it is perceived as more directional whereas the Rose Quartz is more diffuse.

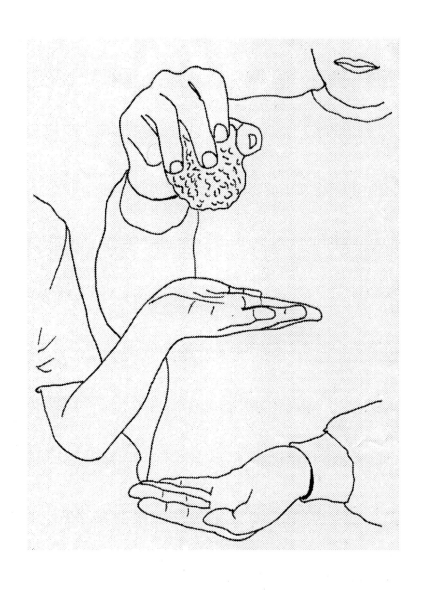

DIAGRAM 17 - Crystal and Palm Chakra

Crystals can be placed on or around the body for healing and meditation purposes. Personally I have found that both with myself and with my clients, it is usually more than sufficient to place the crystals merely within the auric field rather than on the physical body and I would suggest that it is preferable to work in this way as the effects of crystal healing can be extremely powerful. I also feel that it is generally unnecessary to place them on the body as the process is such that crystal energy generally works initially on the energy body filtering inwards to the physical, therefore, it follows that this is the optimum point to place them.

A simple and effective method of working with crystals in a healing capacity would be to put together a chakra set. Choose crystals, which resonate to the colours of the chakras. Below is a suggested list, they need only be in the form of tumblestones and the size is relatively unimportant.

Primary Chakras
Base: Red Jasper, Ruby, and Garnet.
Sacral: Carnelian, Orange Calcite, and Topaz
Solar Plexus: Citrine, Tigers Eye, and Amber
Heart: Aventurine, Emerald, and Moss Agate
Throat: Blue Lace Agate, Celestite, Aqua Aura, and Blue Calcite
Third Eye: Sodalite, Lapis Lazuli, and Sapphire
Crown: Amethyst, Fluorite, and Clear Quartz

Secondary or "New" Chakras
Base: Selenite, Moonstone, and Pearl
Sacral: Red Calcite, Rhodocrosite, and Rutilated Quartz
Solar Plexus: Gold, Pyrite, and Citrine
Heart: Rose Quartz, Pink Kunzite, and Star Ruby
Throat: Fluorite, Kyanite, and Sapphire
Third Eye: White Kunzite, Pale Smokey Quartz, and Clear Calcite.
Crown: Danburite, Herkimer Diamonds, and Chinese Fluorite

When you have drawn together the crystals you wish to use in your chakra set, cleanse, dedicate and attune them.

If it is possible to use a massage couch or table place the crystals on the floor underneath the "patient" at the position of the chakras. If not, place the crystals at the side of the patient but at the level of each chakra. Then simply either visualise the crystals connecting with each chakra, or draw your hand over each crystal, seeing the energy igniting and flowing into the chakra.

After a few moments remove the crystals and "ground" your patient by placing a suitable grounding crystal such as Hematite, Snowflake Obsidian or Black Tourmaline at the feet of the "patient".

This technique should help to balance and energise the chakra system. You can check the effectiveness by dowsing the chakras before placing the crystals and then dowsing them again after the crystals have been removed.

Crystals lend themselves beautifully to being set in jewellery. It is important to remember that if you wear a particular piece of jewellery frequently it needs to be regularly cleansed in order that it can continue to aid the energy field.

It is preferable to wear only the crystals that you feel you need, as combining a variety of crystals may be counter-productive, due to different energetic "messages" being given out from each crystal.

You can also carry stones in your pocket or even bras for a similar effect! Wearing rings can help to stimulate the meridians on particular fingers and wearing earrings can aid in aligning the energetic field surrounding the head, throat and neck. The level of the chain for pendants obviously will have some bearing on the placement of the crystal and could

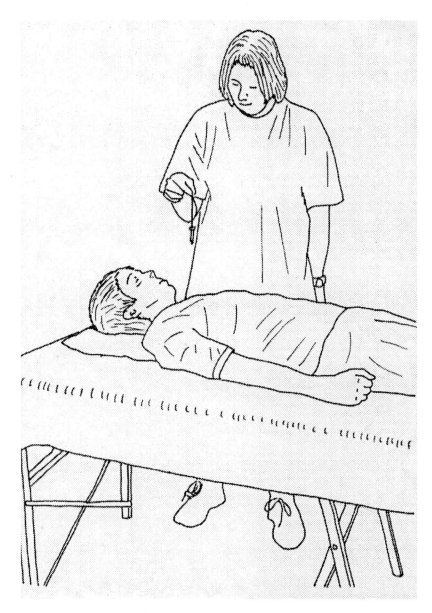

DIAGRAM 18 - Chakra dowsing.

therefore affect either the throat, heart or solar plexus depending on the length of the chain.

Crystals are a very creative way of using natural energy to heal and enhance our lives. The way that we can work with them and incorporate them into our lives are endless and bound only by the limitations of our own imagination. All that is needed is a little time and patience combined with an initially open mind for the connection with this particular type of natural energy to be achieved.

5. Light and Colour Healing - How These Forces Combine to Affect the Surroundings in Which We Live and Favourable Effects Upon Our Well-Being

Colour is something that we take for granted, but try to imagine a world which reflected the colours of black, white and grey like a black and white movie. With no variety of shades and hues of different colours, the world we live in would be more mundane. Light is made up of colour and without light there would be no life. Without colour in our world, there would be no contrast or differences.

Colours encourage order and signals within the natural world. Animals and insects are instinctively drawn to and away from specific plants and creatures by the colours that they display as a form of enticement, warning or even camouflage. They protect the natural world, ensuring that each species continue.

As humans, we react just as instinctively to colour. We are

attracted to some colours and yet repelled by others. We discern light through the medium of colour and it can affect us dramatically. If you measure a person's blood pressure after they had been exposed to a red coloured light for 5 minutes, you would find that it had risen. Change to a blue light for 5 minutes and the blood pressure will fall to the original level.

Colour affects the cell behavior of all bio-chemical structures. Colour therapy practitioners believe that they can treat a variety of ailments from the now well documented Seasonal Affective Disorder (SAD) through to more serious and persistent conditions. Yellow, for instance, helpful for arthritis sufferers, Turquoise rejuvenates cell structures and aids immunity. Green can destroy harmful cells and is useful for conditions such as cancer.

Colour can be a powerful influence on human mood, emotions and atmosphere. A small room painted red will look much smaller than it really is, but paint it blue and it will appear to be much larger.

In a blue room time will seem to pass more slowly whereas in a red room, it is the opposite again. A blue dining room is unlikely to aid digestion and a red bedroom could help to spice up your sex life!

Colour produces chemical changes in the molecular structure of your body, for example blue vibrates about 8 trillion times each second while red vibrates at about two thirds of this speed so all these common expressions such as 'feeling blue' or 'seeing red' or 'green with envy' are actually an articulate description of changes that are taking place in our bodily field of electro-magnetic energies.

In colour healing, the following spectrum of colours are sometimes known as rays.

RED/ORANGE/YELLOW/GREEN/BLUE/INDIGO/VIOLET

An exercise you could try is to have several pieces of material in individual colours. With your eyes closed, try to identify the colour you have in your hand by its energy. Vicky Wall, the creator of Aura Soma products was blind and initially became interested in colour because she was aware of what colour she was in touch with even though she couldn't see it. The ability to sense the difference in colours vibrationally is brought about by the fact that each colour vibrates at a different molecular frequency which with practice and sensitivity, can be felt by anyone.

Here is a summary of the accepted psychological meanings and effects of the main colours:

Dark Blue: confident, conservative, responsible, reliable, tranquil, introspective, discerning, intuitive intelligent and wise.

Light Blue: Peaceful, loving, affectionate, idealistic, communicative, sincere, creative, possessing will power.

Blue-Green: sophisticate, creative, egocentric, fussy, orderly.

Green: peaceful, loyal balance, generous, stable, sensitive, endearing, tenacious.

Yellow-Green: perceptive, non-judgmental, and fearful.

Yellow: cheerful, enthusiastic, intelligent, powerful, optimistic, competitive, variable.

White: neat, orderly, critical, self-sufficient, cautious, motivated, spiritual, positive.

Grey: Tranquil, aloof, and guarded.

Black: sophisticated, serious, authoritative, dramatic, dignified, secure, mystifying, death, and the unknown.

Beige: well adjusted, balanced, hardworking, reliable, honest.

Brown: passive, receptive, loyal, homespun, sense of duty, hardworking, and toiling/drudgery.

Orange: warm, creative, joyful, immediate, assertive, expressive, sexual.

Pink: loving, relaxed, warm-hearted, and maternal.

Red: energetic, sensual, successful, impulsive, restless, extroverted, impatient, and intense.

Purple: spiritual, sensitive, intuitive, open-minded, welcoming.

Violet: intricate, mystical, unifying, enchanting.

The business world places a lot of faith in the ability of colour to encourage us to buy a particular product and a great deal of financial resource is given to the colours which are most appropriate for the packaging of new products, the interior design of a new store and so on.

We do not only connect with colour through sight. It is possible to work with colour by wearing clothing in a specific colour. In this way, our bodies act as a 'filter' and we can absorb the colour internally. This is a very simple way to bring colour into our lives.

Another way to make colour work for you is to select the colour you paint rooms so that it is complementary to the uses that the room will be put to. E.g.:

RED: Use in rooms where there is a high level of physical activity not rooms where you wish to relax and unwind in.

ORANGE: Again, not really appropriate for rooms that are to be used to relax in but good for rooms where a lot of social activity and gathering takes place.

YELLOW: Good to be used in rooms where work is to be done such as writing, thinking, reading, working from home etc. Encourages animated conversation.

GREEN: Encourages an atmosphere of calmness and tranquility but is not conducive to objective or analytical pastimes.

SKY BLUE: Soothing and restful, it is an appropriate colour for bedrooms or kitchens.

INDIGO: Not suitable for rooms where there would be a lot of physical activity or entertaining but ideal for a room where you would meditate or sit to be inspired in such ways as writing, painting etc.

VIOLET/PURPLE: Not suitable again for entertaining but very similar to the uses that you could put the Indigo room to such as contemplation, meditation etc.

The effects of colour in surroundings is being explored in institutions such as prisons and hospitals where cells and wards are painted in colours which are said to engender the correct emotional/physical responses i.e. using a soft green in a hospital ward to promote healing or blue in cells to maintain an atmosphere of calmness and serenity.

The following is a meditation which can be used to balance and re-energise the chakras.

Sit or lie comfortably in a place where you will not be disturbed. If liked, you can burn a candle and incense or oil.

Taking three deep breaths in and sighing out, take your awareness to the Base Chakra situated in the lumber region of the body. Start to see that centre drawing the colour red to it. See it start to be full of vibrant red, allow the red to become intense and imagine the red filling that energy centre. As the centre becomes full, balanced and energised, allow the colour to flow out around the body into the auric field. See a layer of red surrounding the outer edges of the physical body.

Next take your attention to the Sacral Chakra. Start to see the colour orange being drawn to this centre. Be aware of the colour filling up the centre and try to imagine the colour in your mind's eye. As this centre become full, allow the colour to flow out of the chakra and into the auric field, creating a layer of orange around the red layer.

Focus next on the Solar Plexus, drawing Yellow into this centre until it also becomes energised, balanced and aligned. Breathe this colour into the Solar Plexus and visualise the colour being taken throughout the body via the Meridian system. As the centre becomes full, allow the colour to flow into the aura and form another layer around the orange.

Take your awareness to the Heart Chakra. Seeing that centre drawing in light green, imagining the green flowing into the centre and clearing and rebalancing the chakra until it is completely healthy. Then allowing the colour to flow out again into the aura and form another layer around the yellow.

Concentrating next on the Throat Chakra. Drawing the colour Light Blue to that centre and visualising the chakra becoming balanced and aligned with the colour as it flows into the chakra.

When you 'feel' that it is full allow the colour to merge into the aura forming a layer upon the light green.

The next Chakra to focus on is the Brow or 3rd Eye Chakra. Try to imagine drawing the colour Indigo or Deep Blue to this centre and begin to feel the colour flowing into this place. As it becomes complete and whole with the Indigo, allow the colour to flow into the aura and form a layer upon that of the light blue.

Finally, taking your awareness to the Crown Chakra at the top of the head and drawing violet or white to this centre. Allow the centre to balance and draw this colour into itself. As the colour fills the Crown, see it flow out into the aura and form another layer of purple or white upon that of the Indigo.

Try to take your awareness now to the whole picture of the chakras and the aura. If you feel that a particular colour is still not vibrant enough, send out the thought that it should become more energised.

Then breathing more deeply and bringing your focus back into the room, return your awareness to your feet and hands and, when you are ready, opening your eyes.

As you become more adept at this exercise you may feel the need to only 'work' on 1 or 2 specific chakras to form a shorter meditation.

Another way of working with colour in meditation is to focus on something which is the source of the colour or colours that you need at that moment in time. The following is a list, which may help with visualisation:-

WHITE: Candle light, clouds, snow, stars, Clear quartz, and snowdrops

VIOLET: Lavender, Violets (flowers), and Amethyst

INDIGO: Midnight sky, Sodalite

LIGHT BLUE: Sunny Sky, Blue Lace Agate, Cornflower, and Water

PINK: Apple blossom, Rose Quartz

GREEN: Grass, Trees, Aventurine, Limes, Forest

YELLOW: Sunflowers, Field of corn, Lemons, Topaz, and Sunlight

ORANGE: Sunset, Oranges, and Carnelian

RED: Poppies, Roses, Sunset, and Red Jasper

Colour practitioners train for at least two years and they work with a variety of uses of colour such as wearing colour, eating foods made up of specific colours, using light and colour with lamps, visualisation of colour, colour in décor, counselling and analysis using methods such as those pioneered by Dr Max Luscher, a Professor of Psychology who devised a personality test based on the theory that a person's colour preferences were related to the "emotional value" of each colour and thus gave an indication of the basic personality traits.

Modern Medicine is beginning to apply the benefits of healing with colour for several illnesses such as neonatal jaundice, migraine, cancer as well as conditions such as Dyslexia where some people find that certain colours such as pink, blue, yellow or green, when used to make glasses, aid their ability to read by focussing the words more clearly. Research into this phenomena is continuing but my own experience of this was generated by my son who is Dyslexic. His ability to read and focus on words which apparently "shift" as he tries to read them was dramatically improved upon the introduction of yellow glasses.

The therapy was initiated by Goethe, Babbitt, Rudolf Steiner and Ghadiali and more recently Vicky Wall (Aura Soma), Theo Gimbel, Max Luescher, Faber Birren and Mikhael Aivanhov.

Colour healing is still a relatively new therapy, which is beginning to increase in acceptance and lends itself perfectly to anyone wishing to explore the subtle energies, which surround us. It is a therapy which is accessible to all of us and which we can use on a daily basis simply when we decide what colour clothes we are going to wear or what colour foods we are going to eat, for example.

Companies specialising in home decorating products such as paint are now incorporating the therapeutic effects of the particular colours they offer, i.e. whether the colour promotes a tranquil, restful feeling or energises the room if used to paint a particular area in the home, obviously a factor which should be taken into account when choosing what colours to paint various rooms within the home or workplace.

This is a therapy which is easily incorporated into our daily lives and which we can utilise relatively cheaply. More information can be obtained by contacting The International Association of Colour at 46 Cottenham Road, Histon, Cambridge, CB4 9ES.

6. Earth Energies - Leylines, Geopathic Stress, and Crop Circles

The whole area of earth energies regarding ley lines , geopathic stress and so on is a very contentious subject. Many theories abound about the whereabouts, methods of detecting and dealing with the aforementioned energies. I therefore hope to keep the information contained on this subject relatively concise and as factual as is possible.

In recent years there has been a surge of interest in the ancient Chinese art of Feng Shui. Feng Shui is defined as "the Chinese system of good and evil influences on the natural surroundings considered when siting and designing buildings". This has led to an increased interest in the western world and nowadays many top companies such as Virgin and Orange for example, employ Feng Shui consultants to advise them on the placement and decoration of their buildings. For the interested amateurs there are many books which describe the different aspects of this art.

The dictionary definition of a ley line is '*a hypothetical straight line connecting prehistoric sites etc.*' The Chinese place great importance on ley lines which they call "dragon paths"

Today, there is a growing interest in the way that ancient man related to his surroundings and there is an increasing awareness that these old civilisations had an understanding of energy contained within the land which they incorporated into the very fabric of their lives via the use of standing stones, megalithic rings, hill forts, water sources, burial plots and later on sacred sites such as churches and cathedrals.

In a book first published in the 1920s called *The Old Straight Track*, an Englishman called Alfred Watkins noted how these places seemed to be linked to each other in a straight line which could be identified by reading maps of specific areas.

One of the most famous in England is the St Michael Line which runs from St Michael's Mount in Cornwall, cutting through the Hurlers stone circle, Glastonbury Tor, Avebury until it reaches Bury St Edmunds.

It is possible to detect these energies via dowsing either with a pendulum or with metal rods. Where the subject becomes contentious is that experts disagree about the creation of these lines. Did the ancients pick up on already existing energetic lines and build upon them? Did Iron Age man create these lines by building and consecrating the sites that they placed upon them? Or has the energy been allowed to build over the years as a result of these sites being placed upon them.? Some consider that the lines are situated above faults in the rock underground. Maybe it has been a combin-ation of all four which brings us to the point that we are today, where many fascinating theories abound.

Geopathic stress is a term that is becoming more frequently used. It is believed by some that Geopathic stress has four primary causes. The first is shattered energy lines that have been fragmented by mankind's effect upon the environment via buildings and damage to the ecology of earth. In areas of the earth which still lie untouched by man such as the ocean, desert and north pole, these lines are still intact and in their original state.

The secondary cause of geopathic stress is underground water lines. These lines can be subject to a number of fluctuations in their energy, for example the level of the water changes according to the amount of rainfall that we have, it is affected by the changes in temperature of the seasons and by the moon phases which cause it also to ebb and flow. In addition to this, water can become polluted and contaminated. All these changes can have an energetic effect which can cause fluctuations in the levels of energy above ground, this, in turn, can affect us.

The third type of geopathic stress is caused by electro magnetic pollution emitted from modern day technology that we all use and are all subject to. The list is growing and includes mobile phones and their aerials, microwave cookers, power cables, computers and televisions.

The final cause of geopathic stress is considered to by generated by fault lines that emit Radon Gas. Recent research has shown that houses built on land which was previously used as a rubbish tip, have an unacceptable level of this gas in them and there appears to be a link between this gas and the increased chance of ill health in the occupants of these homes.

Many theories abound as to the effects of geopathic stress but most people with knowledge of this subject accept that at the very least it can affect the natural energy levels of the body whilst others feel that it can cause higher incidences of diseases such as Cancer, ME, MS for example.

There are numerous remedies that can help, ranging from plug in appliances to placements of crystals. In the case of computers, microwaves, TVs and so on it is believed that putting a Rose Quartz or Clear Quartz crystal next to the machine will help to alleviate the negative emissions.

This is a subject that is becoming more and more relevant to our lives and the modern day causes of illnesses. Ironically, it may teach us to reconnect again to the wisdom of the ancients and lead us to live more in harmony and with respect for the earth.

Many esoteric folk consider that the earth has its own set of chakras just like the human form and that they are placed at sacred sites around the world. Below is a list of the suggested placements:

Crown Chakra - Mount Kailas in Tibet. This is a site at which Hindus and Buddhists visit and connect with for forgiveness.

3rd Eye Chakra - It is believed that this site is mobile and shifts as the earth passes through new cycles.

Throat Chakra - Great Pyramid in Egypt.

Heart Chakra - Glastonbury. A magical place which is shrouded in mythology as the final resting place of King Arthur and Guinivere, the location where Joseph of Aramathea brought the chalice which was used at the last supper and many other legends.

Solar Plexus Chakra - Ayers Rock (sometimes known as Uluru) in Australia is believed to be a sacred site where all sacred places meet.

Sacral Chakra - Lake Titicaca in South America.

Base Chakra - Mount Shasta in the U.S.A.

Many people are drawn to visit these sites in order to perform earth-healing ceremonies and to connect with the powerful energy vortexes that are found at these places . A good deal of these "pilgrims" do indeed seem to receive intense meditation experiences.

The Aetherius Society, founded by Dr George King in 1955 is a society which promotes spiritual growth and is based in London and Los Angeles. This organisation believes that there are 19 holy mountains which are used as "spiritual batteries". 9 of these mountains are based in Great Britain -

Holdstone Down, North Devon

Old Man, Coniston

Creag-An-Leth-Chain, Cairngorms

Kinderscout, Derbyshire

Pen-Y-Fan, Brecon Beacons

Brown Willy, Bodwin Moor

Yes Tor, Dartmoor, Devon.

Carnedd Llywelyn, Wales

Ben Hope, Scottish Highlands

A final word in this chapter about Crop Circles. These geometric shapes and patterns appear throughout the year in cereal crops, but have also been seen in grass, heather, sand and even ice.

Many theories abound about what or who creates these patterns on the landscape. What is generally accepted is that they seem to appear more frequently near ancient monuments which are on ley lines or points of powerful natural energies. Speculation abounds as to the creators ranging from extra-terrestials, to earth energies although there have been some created by man as hoaxes which do nothing to help the understanding of why and how the vast majority occur.

It is a subject surrounded by myth and conjecture but which continues to fascinate mathematicians, geometers, architects and scientists as well as the layman.

More than 5,000 circles have been documented as appearing world wide and scientific tests have established that there is indeed molecular transformation which takes place within the structure of the plants in addition to an alteration in the chemical composition of the soil. The plants continue to grow and ripen as normal even after they have been effectively flattened to form the pattern.

The study of crop circles continues to fascinate people and many find that as they explore this subject, they experience a deep connection with the patterns and a desire to understand what, why and how these things appear. It is certainly worth a trip to Avebury in Wiltshire, where there is a higher than average proportion of crop circles which appear each year, in order to see this phenomenon.

If you feel drawn to doing some earth healing you can simply visit a sacred site which you are drawn to and meditate using a visualisation to bring energy to this site. Alternatively, you can work with crystals by creating a crystal mandala or grid. Working with the crystals you can form symbol, for example, a six pointed star, a representation of the Kabbalah etc.

Again it is also possible to dowse these energies and this can add an extra dimension to a visit to a sacred or historical site.

7. Numerology

Numerology is a system that has evolved over thousands of years and is based on a unique formula. By working out the key number combinations, which are represented by your name and date of birth, Numerology can be used to give an insight into your characteristics and opportunities in life.

It can reveal much information about your potential, health, career and relationships.

The origin of Numerology is not known exactly, however, the Hindus, Hebrews, Egyptians, Greeks and Christians are among those who used this science.

Pythagoras, the Greek mathematician and philosopher, is often thought to be the father of Numerology. Using geometry and secret knowledge gained during his extensive travels, he allocated characteristics to each number. His method of interpreting numbers has been updated through the ages, until it has reached its present stage of development.

Numerologists believe that we are born on a specific date and adopt or are given, a particular name in order to perform a special mission in life and to learn certain lessons. For an accurate assessment your whole name registered after birth is used and it MUST be accurate. The EXACT date of birth is also essential.

Numerology can help you to develop and try to use your potential more effectively, avoiding cul de sacs and frustration. If you have or have had obstacles to overcome, these can be explained. Understanding yourself is a key to both personal and spiritual growth as well as accessing the highest potential of happiness and success open to you.

Numerology can be applied to gain a further understanding of relationships, chosen occupations, children, health, business names, product making, decision making. It can tell you about your purpose in life, character potential, timing, challenges, inner desires, karmic patterns.

General Rules
The full date of birth is required to work out the Life number i.e. remember to include the 19 in the year of birth.

If the full name has more than 4 names, only use the first and the last name. Ignore the others.

If the name is hyphenated, ignore the hyphen and use as two separate names e.g. Mary-Anne should be regarded as Mary Anne.

Combine a compound last name into one name e.g. De La Tour = Delatour.

Don't include appendages such as Sir, Junior, Senior, III, Mr., Mrs., etc.

Key Definitions of Numbers
Note: Unless we are completely enlightened beings it is extremely unusual for us to be entirely in harmony with all aspects of our lives. *Therefore the definitions given for each number include examples of the characteristics thrown up if*

the person has still to develop particular aspects as well as the positive characteristics which can and should be achieved.

I have also enclosed a list of crystals whose vibration is compatible with the particular number. It may be that by working with the crystals through healing techniques, meditation or simply by wearing them in the form of jewellery they can help to bring about a balancing or realigning effect, should you consider it necessary.

Number 1
Underdeveloped - Timid, insecure, under-confident, Shy

Balanced - Self-reliant, Assured, Positive, Initiatory, Pioneer

Overdeveloped - Over-assertive, Bossy, Obstinate, Immovable

Crystal: Moss Agate, Aquamarine, Copper, Turquoise.

Number 2
Underdeveloped - Timid, impressionable, anxious, too sensitive

Balanced: Able to work well with others, tactful, efficient, and empathetic

Overdeveloped - Stand-offish, unfeeling, gossip, sly, chatterbox

Crystals: Fluorite, Garnet, and Gold

Number 3
Underdeveloped - Timid, awkward, fussy, moaner, miserable

Balanced - Happy, artistic, eloquent, articulate, friendly, outgoing

Overdeveloped - Pretentious, bombastic, scandalmonger, vain, chaotic and disorganized

Crystals: Amber, Amethyst, Aventurine, and Lapis Lazuli

Number 4
Underdeveloped - Idle, obstinate, undecided, boring

Balanced - Efficient, hard working, reliable, well-organized, methodical, rational

Overdeveloped - Immovable, curt, argumentative, violent, obstinate, and headstrong.

Crystals: Apophyllite, Danburite, and Emerald

Number 5
Underdeveloped - Idle, headstrong, uncertain, boring

Balanced - Busy, adaptable, communicator, charismatic, forceful, energetic

Overdeveloped - Untrustworthy, reckless, excessive, inconsistent, careless, impetuous, irresponsible.

Crystals: Blue Lace Agate, Touchstone,

Number 6
Underdeveloped - Thoughtless, inconsiderate, apathetic, untrustworthy, careless, not sensitive to others

Balanced - Affectionate, giving, aesthetic, unpretentious, responsible, warm, caring, artistic

Overdeveloped - Over-enthusiastic, excessively sensitive, antagonistic, bitter, highly strung, gives too much of themselves

Crystals: Citrine, Jasper, Marble, Apache Tear, and Onyx

Number 7
Underdeveloped - Detached, unpredictable, chaotic, insecure

Balanced - Explorative, perceptive, self-reliant, curious, competent, independent, logical, rational, thorough

Overdeveloped - Antisocial, too distinct, alienated, obsessive, solitary, unfriendly, hostile

Crystals: Flint, Kunzite, Pearl, Platinum, and Rose Quartz

Number 8
Underdeveloped - Unrealistic, vulnerable, disordered, weak, delicate

Balanced: Active, capable, self-assured, forceful, vital, competent, effective, confidant

Overdeveloped - Over-confident, selfish, misuses power, self centered, self indulgent

Crystals: Fossil, Jet, Snowflake Obsidian, Opal, and Selenite

Number 9
Underdeveloped: Confined, vulnerable, avaricious, vindictive, narrow minded, weak, greedy

Balanced: Liberal, altruistic, idealistic, tolerant, unselfish, humane, charitable, forgiving

Overdeveloped - Daydreamer, unreliable, over idealistic, self pitying

Crystals: Chalcedony, Geode, Hematite, and Malachite

Number 11/2: Master Number
Underdeveloped - See balanced 2

Balanced - Idealist, inspired, powerful, capable, able to "see the bigger picture"

Overdeveloped - Romanticist, drifting or extreme, misuses power

Crystals: Jade

Number 22/4: Master Number
Underdeveloped - See balanced 4

Balanced - Very able, sensible, influential, efficient, orderly, dynamic, forceful

Overdeveloped - Rigid, egotistical, misuses power, nervous, arrogant, empty headed

Crystals: Coral

Working Out Your Life Mission Number

This number will give you an indication of your life's purpose and the direction in which you should be heading. It can indicate typical characteristics and it is the most powerful single factor indicating the potential that the particular individual is able to achieve.

If you are feeling personally dissatisfied with life, it may be that you have not yet developed or expressed your life's mission and by identifying the potential you may be able to become a more contented, balanced and successful person in the relevant areas of your life that are currently lacking.

Using the FULL date of birth, add together each component of the date of birth and then reduce.

E.g.: Date of birth 21 June 1938

21 - 6 - 1938
= 2+1 - 6 - 1+9+3+1
= 3   6   14
= 5   6   1+4
= 5   6   5

Next step is the add the numbers together and then if necessary, reduce again

E.g. $5 + 6 + 5 = 16 = 1 + 6 = 7$ = Life Path Number

Your name can also be "worked out" numerologically using the following chart. The "vibration" of your name is reflected in the final number that is achieved after adding up the total. This chart can also be used to analyse the effectiveness of house names, business titles, company names etc.

1	2	3	4	5	6	7	8	9
A	B	C	D	E	F	G	H	I
J	K	L	M	N	O	P	Q	R
S	T	U	V	W	X	Y	Z	

Working out the name numerologically gives us an indication of the following traits and attributes:

How you communicate and connect with everyone

Shows what you are really like, pulls away the veneers that we place around ourselves to provide a deeper understanding of the real you.

Can give an indication of a suitable career.

May give clues as to what motivates you.

It may be an interesting exercise to work out the names and dates of well known people and see if you can recognize any aspects within their number makeup.

It may also be an interesting exercise to work out the changes which may be brought about by factors such as marriage, titles, the application of formal name as opposed to informal names such as James to Jim as well as nicknames etc.

When working out business names it is also a good idea to consider the date that the business is started on as a substitute for date of birth for example.

Finally, it may be interesting to explore the implications of the numbers of people who play important roles in your lives in comparison to your numbers. It may be a simple as slightly changing a name and thereby a number enables you to relate better to someone close to you.

8. Plant Energies - Working With Plants and Trees Including Making Homeopathic Remedies, Flower Essences and How to Make a Vibrational Spray

Nature with all of its creations provides us with a myriad of raw materials from which we can produce individual vibrational healing tools, materials and medicines. We have ingredients such as herbs, flowers, wood, leaves, crystals and so on from which to concoct recipes based on ancient folklore, intuition, or the many alternative medicine books which are available today.

Working with the natural energies of plants, flowers and trees can be a powerful experience if you can attune yourself fully to the energies that they hold.

Many people are now moving away from the idea of the body being purely a mechanical vehicle whose breakdown can be analysed simply by looking at the parts which have become broken and fixing or replacing them.

Nowadays we are becoming more aware of the emotional, mental and spiritual tolls that play a part in the disruption of the physical.

This growing awareness has led to the greater acceptance of "vibrational" remedies. By the term "vibrational" healers we mean working with the intrinsic energy of a crystal, plant, flower piece of wood etc. This energy or vibration is difficult to show but with perseverance and attunement, it is possible to "connect" with the energy by different methods such as dowsing or simply sitting quietly with the selected item in your hand and feeling the energy which may simply feel like a slight "buzzing" or vibration. If these methods do not allow you to connect, just try working with them, keeping a record of the condition that you are trying to alter. Remember, most vibrational medicine is extremely subtle and can take up to several days for the effects to be felt. This is due to the remedy working initially on the auric field before finally filtering through into the physical. Therefore the healing effect may not be immediate.

Another point to note, when working with all forms of healing but especially with vibrational healing, is that the initial effects of the remedy may not be perceived as positive. As we discussed in Chapter 1, vibrational healers know these reactions as healing crises or responses and although in some cases it may not feel very positive at the time, most practitioners regard this as an indication that energetic "blocks" are being released. When receiving treatment of this kind, it is important to try to determine whether the treatment feels "right" to you. The first time I was aware of a healing crisis, I experienced flu like symptoms that went almost as quickly as they arrived within a few hours. During that time I was forced to "opt out" of my busy life and was able to take time to reflect on the treatment and the situation I was being treated for. I felt very aware on an intuitive level that the response I was experiencing was O.K.

However, as with all treatment it is important to use the utmost discernment and when you are unsure or unhappy with the results of treatment to take the time to consult your practitioner.

In the next few paragraphs, I hope to encourage you to begin to work with these energies and to take steps towards creating your own remedies. However, remember that these remedies are not a replacement for medical treatment and should be used in conjunction with advice from your GP

In *The Fragrant Heavens* Valerie Ann Wormwood identifies the following oils as suitable to work with specific chakras.

Crown:- Frankincense, Neroli, Rose

Brow:- Angelica Seed, Hyacinth, Juniper, Lemon, Pine, Rosemary

Throat:- Basil, Chamomile, Cypress, Hyssop, Linden Blossom, Peppermint, Petitgrain, Rosemary, Rosewood

Heart:- Bergamot, Geranium Jasmine, Lavender, Mandarin, Melissa, Rose Maroc, Tangerine, Ylang Ylang.

Solar Plexus: Black Pepper, Cardamom, Cedarwood, Coriander, Hyssop, Juniper, Lime, and Marjoram.

Sacral: - Benzoin, Cardamom, Clary Sage, Fennel, and Sandalwood.

Base:- Balsam de Peru, Myrrh, Patchouli, Rosewood, Thyme, Vetiver.

I have worked both personally and with groups checking the effectiveness of these oils upon the chakras by dowsing for imbalances and then placing a two or three drops of oil on a tissue which is then laid lightly upon the chakra point. If you use dowsing it is possible to perceive a change in the energy of the chakra being brought about by the introduction of the oil.

Essential oils can be used to make chakra sprays by adding to water and putting into a spray container. If you are a proficient dowser you may find it interesting to dowse the energy of the solution from the start, through each stage as you progress adding various oils. You can dowse each oil for its appropriateness for use, the number of drops required and the effect that it has upon the spray after it has been added.

If you have access to a natural spring, the energetic quality of the spray will be enhanced by using this rather than ordinary tap water or failing this, buy a good quality spring water from your local supermarket. You may also wish to add a teaspoon or so of alcohol in order to preserve the spray.

Alternatively you can use your own intuition to decide which oils you would use to create a spray which is individual to yourself, referring to the list of oils at the beginning of this chapter, or using others that you may be drawn to. In addition to adding the essential oils, it is possible to add crystal energy via the following method:

Hold a previously cleansed crystal in the left hand that you have selected for its energetic properties. A good general choice is for example Rose Quartz.

In the right hand hold a crystal point or termination with the point aimed at the spray bottle.

Taking your focus to the crystal in your right hand, connect with its energy and visualise the energy travelling up the arm on the in breath. On the second in breath, visualise the energy being held in the heart chakra. On the third in breath send the energy down the right arm, through the crystal and into the spray. Do this exercise three times and if you wish to you can dowse the spray to see how the energy has changed.

Use the spray whenever you feel it is appropriate by spraying into the auric field, but take care not to spray on polished wood or furnishing materials and clothes, as the oils may leave a residue.

The technique to transfer crystal energy can also be used to energise water, food, furniture, jewellery and so on.

Attuning yourself to the energies of flowers, trees and plants is not difficult but can sometimes look a bit odd to the uninitiated in these things.

A good example is to try to sense the difference in energy compared between a healthy and unhealthy plant that is wilting. You will find that the life force on the healthy plant is much stronger than the unhealthy and this can be picked up either by dowsing or sensing the energy with the hands as we did previously when working on the human aura. Some people are also able to see the energy in a similar way to that of our own auras.

It is possible to sense the energy field of a tree by simply standing with your hands outstretched. Allow yourself to become still and centered in much the same way as you do when preparing to sense the human energy field. Again the way that the tree's energy field feels is very individual to the person. It may be that they can sense a connection on an intuitive level with the tree, they may become aware of a magnetic field surrounding the tree or they may find that the connection is more subtle and that it affects the mood or emotional state that they are in.

Next time you go for a walk in nature, through woods or simply in your garden try to be aware of how you are feeling before and then monitor your feelings after you have come away from the environment. It's generally accepted that you will feel in a more relaxed and positive frame of mind afterwards. Nature exists in a state of unconditional love which can be tapped into purely by buying a beautiful bunch of flowers and displaying them in your home so it is possible for even the most urban of flat dwellers to connect with this generous loving energy.

Flower Remedies are becoming more and more readily available and accepted. They really deserve a chapter all of their own. These are very much archetypal vibrational tools originally created by Edward Bach, who had a successful medical career, but gave it up to refine and create the 38 Bach Flower Remedies which have been in use since 1936. These remedies are prepared in much the same way as homeopathic medicines.

The 38 remedies are based on what he identified as 38 negative emotional states. Dr Bach felt that it was important that he treat the person and so great emphasis was placed, when diagnosing on identifying exactly what the emotions are that you are feeling and then selecting a Remedy based on the emotion.

Today there are literally hundreds of Flower Remedies, Gem Essences, and Tree Essences and so on to choose from. They are completely safe to take and can work on a vibrational level to alleviate any emotion that becomes too uncomfortable for us to experience. Of the many newer versions there are many which are said to also help promote spiritual growth and understanding.

If you wish to make your own, it is a simple process but one which needs the creator to have a strong affinity with and respect for nature. This procedure will be enhanced through practice and attunement.

In selecting the flower that we wish to work with, it is important to open up the intuition and start to communicate with the plant, in order to become aware of the qualities which it offers freely.

For example, a rose may provide unconditional love whilst a daisy may bring the quality of simplicity to the flower remedy. You may disagree with these suggestions as you connect with similar flowers and if this is the case, accept your own interpretation.

In order to begin to create a flower essence, stand in the garden and try to notice whether you are drawn to a particular plant. Stand close to the plant and notice which flowers are 'calling' you. It is said that the plant will allow the flowers you need to come to you to be plucked easily so if you are still at a stage where you find it difficult to trust your own intuition, notice if the flowers come away easily and if you find that they are becoming more difficult to detach, take it as a sign that the plant has given enough.

Place the flowers face down in a glass bowl or dish of spring water, preferably about half an inch deep, covering the surface. This ensures that the energy within the water will be extremely concentrated.

The container should then be placed in the sun, ideally next to the plant if possible. Ask that the deva or spirit of the plant bless the water with its energy and qualities. The container should be left to absorb direct sunlight for at least three hours or even longer if it is not a very sunny day. Dowsing can be an excellent way of deciding when this process has been completed.

Next, remove the flowers, preferably with a leaf so as not to contaminate the water with any other energy and mix an equal amount of alcohol such as brandy or vodka with the water. This acts as a preservative but it is important to realise that the mixture is now energised with the spirit of the plant and that it needs to be respected. Place this 'Mother Tincture' aside for a few days to allow it to adapt.

After a few days have elapsed, fill a 10ml bottle with a mixture of spring water and alcohol and add up to 7 drops from the Mother Tincture to the 'Stock Bottle'. In order to preserve the stock bottle for a long time, you need to ensure that at least half of the liquid is alcohol but equally important is that you use spring water to keep the essence 'alive'.

Some people who make essences believe that it is important at this stage to allow the stock bottle to rest in close proximity to the mother tincture in order for the remedy to slowly attune itself again to the change in it's surroundings. After a few days it is ready for use.

The dosage should be 2 drops from the stock bottle added to about 1 oz of spring water and taken 4 times a day. Alternatively the stock can be rubbed into the body which allows it to work through the auric field.

I personally feel that making an essence using the above steps empowers the remedy far more than the majority of commercially produced flower essences on the market and I would encourage anyone tempted to have a go.

In this chapter, attention has to be drawn to the phenomenal increase in the use of essential oils. These products are primarily intended for external use and should not be placed undiluted on the skin. When using essential oils you should be guided by advice from a qualified Aromatherapist, doctor or an authoritative book on the subject such as those written by Valerie Ann Wormwood.

It is common for people to underestimate the strength and power of the oils and for this reason great care needs to be taken by anyone who is pregnant, suffering from Epilepsy or on a course of prescribed medication.

However, for the uninitiated here is a list of ways of utilising their qualities.

Using a burner, you can heat the oil, which in turn will vaporise and perfume the room, affecting the atmosphere according to the choice of oil. For example, Lavender is said to be relaxing, whilst Rosemary is said to be invigorating and Ylang-Ylang is said to be soothing and sensual. By blending together 2 or 3 drops of particular oils you create what is called a blend or synergy. The ways that each oil interacts with the other brings a vibrancy to the final result.

Bath Oil. Usually, only 5 drops of essential oil added to the bath are sufficient. Before you get into the bath gently stir the water to disperse the oil. As you relax in the bath your body will absorb a small amount of the oil and the remainder will gently evaporate in the heat releasing a beautiful smell.

Massage. Again all that is needed is about 5 drops of essential oil to 10 mils of a massage base such as Sweet Almond Oil which can be purchased very cheaply at your local Pharmacist. This is then massaged into the body (preferably by someone else!) allowing the body to receive the benefits of massage combined with the vibrational healing of the oils.

It is possible to connect with the deva or elemental presence within the oil in much the same way as with a crystal by holding the chosen bottle in the left hand and sitting quietly for a few moments. Empty your mind and allow the unconscious thoughts to filter through. As you feel your connection you may be aware of the energy generating from the bottle and you may experience an emotion, thought or picture in your mind's eye. When this happens, honour and acknowledge the connection. It is important not to just dismiss it as your imagination. If you can do this exercise with friends within a group, you will be surprised at the similarity in perceptions that you all have.

A final word about a more commonly accepted form of vibrational healing - Homeopathy.

Homeopathy was developed over 200 years ago by a German man called Samuel Hahnemann who discovered that by dosing himself with a substance which caused a similar reaction to a particular illness he could bring about a reversal of the symptoms. This was known as *"similia similibus curentur"* or 'like may be cured by like'.

So, in order to cure malaria, the patient would be prescribed quinine, which in a healthy person would manifest the same symptoms, but the patient suffering from malaria would be cured. Hahnemann fine tuned the process so that the dosages would be appropriate to each patient, but to his surprise he discovered that as he diluted them, the medicines began to work more quickly and effectively. Today the doses are measured and prescribed in centesimal potencies.

We can duplicate on a crude level an Amethyst crystal homeopathic remedy by the following method:

Place an Amethyst crystal in alcohol for 2 days, this becomes known as the Mother Tincture. Take one drop of this liquid (which you can store in a bottle for use again) and mix it with 99 drops of alcohol and tap or "succuss" the remedy - traditionally this was done on a Bible and usually for 100 times Again take one drop of this liquid and mix it again with 99 more drops of alcohol and so on.

The dilution is measured in 6c by a dilution 6 times by a factor of 100 and 30c is dilution of 30 times a factor of 100. In other words, the process described above has been repeated in the case of a 6c potency 6 times and each time the remedy has been tapped or "succussed" 100 times.

The final solution can then be added to lactose pills, tablets or granules and taken as required.

The most commonly used potencies are 6c and 30c. 6c being the potency most commonly used in less acute and 30c being the potency used in more chronic conditions.

The final Amethyst remedy would be suitable for use to enhance meditation and clear-sightedness.

Working with the powers of nature is a simple and effective method of allowing the intrinsic healing abilities of plants, herbs and crystals and so on to aid us in realigning and balancing the vital life force within us.

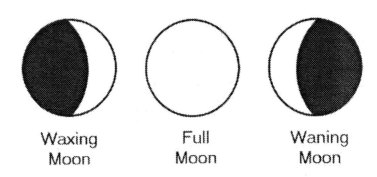

	Waxing Moon	Full Moon	Waning Moon

Date	Celtic Festival	Christian Festival
1 May	Beltane	Whitsun
21 June	Midsummer Solstice	St John's Feast
1 August	Lughnasa	Lammas
23 September	Autumn Equinox	Harvest Festival
1 November	Samhain	All Souls, All Saints
21 December	Midwinter Solstice	Christmas
2 February	Imbolc	St Brigid's Candlemas
23 March	Vernal Equinox	Easter

DIAGRAM 19 - Moon Phases

9. Solar and Lunar Energy - How the Sun and Moon Affects Us

Thousands of years ago man looked to the earth but also to the sky for his spiritual understanding. Pagans, Druids and Native Americans Indians, all incorporated the sun and the moon into their belief systems as do many other civilisations. The ancient Egyptians for example worshipped the Sun God Ra and the Moon Goddess Isis.

The sun is commonly regarded as representing the masculine aspect whilst the moon represents the feminine.

The moon's constantly changing state from one cycle to the next draws obvious parallels to that of the female menstrual cycle but also to the phases of womanhood: i.e. Maiden, Mother, and Crone.

Although the moon may be continually changing, the cycle remains constant. It is one of new growth, fruition and decline.

If we link our spiritual understanding to the moon phases we can come to understand that there may be a relevance to incorporating these phases within our day to day lives as did the ancients.

New Moon: This is seen as a time to cleanse but also a time to create. An auspicious time to initiate new ideas, projects or goals. It is regarded as a good time for retreat and meditation.

It is also common for people to feel sad or depressed around this time.

Full Moon: This is the time to harvest what you have sown. Witches would use this phase as the optimum time to cast their spells!

Waning Moon: This is a time of release and reassessment. A time to let go of outmoded patterns, relationships etc.

Pagan Moon Rituals By Month

These rituals should take place at the most relevant phase of the moon.

January: Protection - plan a ritual or focus on protection centering around the home and family. Tree Month - Rowan, symbolising life

February: Future - take time out to think about the future. Tree Month - Ash, symbolising sea power.

March: Initiation - focus on what you would wish for the future and plan a ritual or mediation on or around those wishes. Tree Month - Alder, symbolising Fire.

April: Planting - start to sow the seeds of whatever you desire. Perhaps even planting real seeds as a physical representation of those desires. Tree Month - Willow, symbolising enchantment.

May: Reaffirmation - meditate on or create a ritual to reaffirm the goals. Tree Month - Hawthorn, symbolising purification.

June: Balance - take time to think about drawing together your physical and spiritual needs. Tree Month - Oak, symbolising triumph.

July: Acknowledgement - think about or create a ritual or meditation on what you will do and how you will feel when your needs have been achieved. Tree Month - Holly, symbolising the waning year

August: Consolidation - decide how best to preserve and retain what you have already. Tree Month - Hazel, symbolising wisdom.

September: Harvesting - focus on giving thanks for the fruition of your plans. Tree Month - Vine, symbolising joy and anger.

October: Thanksgiving - take stock of what you have received over the past few months and give thanks. Tree Month - Ivy, symbolising resurrection

November: Cleansing - create a meditation or ritual on cleansing and removing any negative thoughts or vibrations. Tree Month - Reed, symbolising established power.

December: Strength - reassert your convictions and meditate on how to remain steadfast. Tree Month - Mistletoe, symbolising virility.

Throughout the years, man has looked to the sun as a source of life-giving light and warmth. It is apparent to all that when the sun is in decline in winter life is hard. Crops need the warmth and light of the sun to grow and without it, life is not sustainable.

It is easy to see, therefore why man placed such emphasis on the seasonal appearances and disappearances of the sun. The Celts for example, divided their year into celebrations linked these to solar ebbs and flows.

The most important days in the Celtic calendar were Winter Solstice which marked the new beginning, symbolised by the re-birth of the sun. Traditionally, this is the shortest day of the year. The Summer Solstice represents the decline of the sun and although this is the longest day when the sun is furthest north it is also the turning point into winter.

Many theories abound about the uses for stone circles but latter day researchers agree that whatever their functions they seem to be linked to the cycles of the sun. In 1906, Sir Norman Lockyer who was an astronomer and scientist concluded in his publication of *Stonehenge and other British Stone Monuments Astronomically Considered*, that early stone circles such as Stonehenge and New Grange in Ireland, for example, were built to be illuminated by the sunrise or sunset at specific days of the Celtic year. Even though man had only primitive forms of transport available, archaeological evidence shows that great importance was placed upon these circles to the extent that many people traveled to these points at the appropriate time of year in order to see the effects brought about by the sunrises and sunsets.

Working with the earth's natural cycles such as sunsets, sunrises, seasons and the movements of the moon allows us to reaffirm a connection with our world and it's surroundings.

This connection is important if we are to sustain life on this planet for ourselves and future selves as well as all of the other inhabitants - animal, vegetable and mineral.

10. Meditation, A Deeper Perspective - Devas, Angels, Guides and Ascended Masters

As you work through some or all of the exercises in this book it is almost inevitable that you will find that you are able to connect on a deeper spiritual level in a way that is individual to you. Most people, as they grow spiritually, find that their sensitivity to various energies become more pronounced. One person may find that they are increasingly drawn to use crystals and that they are much more aware of the energies and the benefits, which they can obtain from working with this particular therapy. Another person may find that their ability to dowse becomes extremely accurate or that they have started to have a greater awareness of the energies of others and may begin to develop clairvoyant tendencies.

Every person is an individual and his or her development is usually reflected in an extremely personal way. This is why I find that when I am teaching psychic awareness it is far better to encourage my groups to do experiential exercises than to talk about the theory and possible responses that they can expect to get as their personal growth increases. Also, whilst it is perfectly O.K. to work through the exercises within this book alone, far more can be gained by carrying out the exercises in a group environment whether it is with like-minded friends or in a more formal setting. The feedback which you provide each other following the exercises, can offer confirmation of a response which you may have rejected as purely your imagination, support and understanding when a healing response is experienced as well as detached viewpoints as to the experiences of individual members and suggestions and discussions on issues raised which may be beneficial to the development of each member of the group. This is why I always recommend that wherever possible you join or form a group of like-minded individuals. This does not mean that you must all "get on". As everyone develops, the dynamics of the group changes and most groups have their "button pushers" who will probably provide the most opportunity for growth to the person whose button is being pushed although they may not see it at the time!

As you progress with meditation, most people find that they begin to experience empowerment within the soul or a greater esoteric awareness. For some this may take the form of a religious connection, perhaps they may feel drawn to understand a particular religion, others may feel that they wish to reject the belief structures that they have held all of their lives up to that point. In other cases it may take the form of rejection of personal relationships with others which are no longer working for the individual or it may simply be just a gentle growth in awareness and a deeper appreciation of something intangible but which they have always been connected with. I would caution against being judgmental of others' paths and development. In my experience, pride usually does come before a fall and we all have very different paths to tread, although we can walk the same paths with others for a while.

I offer the following insights that I have encountered over the years within the groups that I have been fortunate enough to teach and be part of, as illustrations of ways in which experiences during meditation can be identified. These experiences do not "happen" to everyone but seem to be quite common within a cross-section of a group. It is important to keep an open mind and not to "try" too hard to manifest anything. My observations are merely suggestions of what these experiences mean and I would urge you to disregard any suggestion which you consider to be inappropriate and to go with your own or other's interpretations should they feel more "right".

As your ability to meditate becomes more developed you may find that you start to "see" colours with your eyes closed through the 3rd eye chakra. These colours sometimes swirl and change in a slightly psychedelic manner. My personal interpretation is that they can be related to the chakras and may be an indication of healing which is taking place. I frequently 'see' the colour purple and when this happens to me I am aware that I have connected with my Guides whilst when I see a circle of white I feel that I have forged a connection with an angelic influence.

You may find that you become aware of a presence near to you although when you open your eyes there is no one around. Again I feel that this is Guides making their presence felt. As long as the presence feels "positive" and that you are not fearful it may be a good opportunity to "talk" mentally to your Guide, acknowledging and honouring their presence and indicating that you are happy for them to forge a closer connection with you.

You may be aware of words which start to pop into your mind although you are in a state of deep relaxation and the words and phrases may not be the type that you would usually use. This is probably your Guide attempting to "channel" higher guidance through you and as long as you are happy and feel comfortable with this process you can experience a deeper and closer connection by developing this ability.

If you experience anything which you feel is negative or remotely uncomfortable, it is important that you know that you are completely in control and that you can stop whenever you wish. It's at times like these, that it is extremely helpful to have others who you can confide in and who can help to find an overview of the situation in order that you can learn from it and move forward. Sometimes when we experience energies that are different from our own or that which we have become accustomed to, it can feel a little disconcerting or even frightening. At times like these it is imperative that you listen to your inner feelings and respond appropriately.

There are many other experiences which can spontaneously occur during meditation such as out of body experiences, personal insights, clairvoyance, clairaudience and so on. The golden rule is that if it does not feel right discontinue and state your intent to the entities or energies that you have connected with.

We all have free will and it if it feels inappropriate, uncomfortable or frightening then do not allow yourself to be used in this way. Mentally state this and visualise protection and clearing around and throughout your auric and physical bodies and detach.

Finally, in order to end on a positive note I offer you a glossary of positive energies and entities which may seek to connect and work with you in order to aid and support your spiritual growth.

DEVAS - These are generally accepted as being elementals or spiritual beings connected with nature. For example, there may be a Deva connected to a crystal or a flower. Hindus or Buddhists see Devas as gods or goddesses - the word deva literally translates as beings of light.

ANGELS - It may be surprising but there are myriads of different types of angels who seek to build bridges between the spiritual realms and us. As awareness of angels has recently become far greater, there is a good selection of books that seek to illustrate the differences between types of angels and give exercises that can facilitate connections with these beings. They are renowned for not liking negative or noisy spaces but do like flowers, pastel colours and crystals. They communicate with the creative part of our being with the exception of Raphael who is more linked to the logical part of us. The most common contacts may well however be with the following:-

Guardian Angel - usually are spirits which have had incarnations but are currently residing in spirit and are assigned to watch over and guide individuals who are currently incarnate. It is from these beings that you can ask for omens or portents in order to provide you with support, proof or guidance. They are also responsible for karma, past life connections and spiritual philosophy.

Archangels - perceived as neither masculine nor feminine beings who have never incarnated but are spiritual beings who oversea the physical realms as follows:

Michael - Archangel of the South representing Fire. Encompasses protection, strength, courage, sexual desire, hatred, love, passion and understanding.

Gabriel - Archangel of the West representing Water. Encompasses water, moon, goddess energy, dreams, awareness, gentleness, and birth.

Raphael - Archangel of the East representing Air. Encompasses teacher, computers, creativity, poetry, art, healing and communication.

Uriel - Archangel of the North representing Earth. Encompasses earth, stones, devic kingdoms, mystery, darkness.

Azrael - Archangel of the Centre representing the whole. Encompasses akashic records (which are said to be the records of everything that has ever happened), spirit, death and re-birth.

Melchizadeck - Nurturer of all the angelic kingdoms

The White Brotherhood or Ascended Masters. A group of beings who were incarnated usually over more than one lifetime who as a result have become highly evolved and therefore no longer need to incarnate but seek to serve and guide the whole of humanity in their spiritual evolvement. They can connect as group energy or as individuals depending on the wisdom that they wish to impart. The following is a list of some of the masters and what they represent, although it is by no means definitive.

Mother Mary - Gentle energy, nurturing divine mother, loving all beings, feminine power, connected with seasons, birth. Using the colour of Madonna Blue or the smell of roses may enhance the connection with this master.

Jesus - sometimes known as Sananda. Energy is loving, passionate, intense, strong, clear, aligned to truth and wisdom, expanding the consciousness and aiding manifest-ation. Using the colour of red and smells of nutmeg or ginger may enhance connection with this master.

Lady Nada - was reputed to have been Mary Magdalene in a previous life and is therefore connected to Jesus and Mother Mary on a soul level. Lady Nada brings the qualities of joy, innocence, purity, sensuality, sexuality, inner child connection, solar feminine qualities and connection may be enhanced by the smell of jasmine and the colour pink.

Kathumi - Reputed to have had an incarnation as Francis of Assisi. Comes in on a yellow ray and is linked to the animal, crystal and earth kingdoms as well as representing vital life force, ley lines, vortexes etc. Connection can be aided by floral smells and the colour yellow.

St Germain - Was Francis Bacon, Merlin, Christopher Columbus. Teaches through challenge, ceremony, ritual, affirmation. Linked to the colour of Violet and the smell of Bergamot.

Lady Portia - Soulmate of St Germain. Represented by the dark feminine characters in Shakespeare's plays such as Lady Macbeth. Focuses on endings and beginnings, feminine power that can sometimes be dark and sinister but ultimately achieves a positive ending. Known as the Guardian of the Way, magical and mystical can be linked with through the smells of oranges and lemons and the colour of dark violet.

El Moraya - Incarnated as King Arthur and an Indian prince. Represents equilibrium, leadership, balance, strength, protection, strategy, loyalty, discipline and the masculine manifestation of unconditional love. Linked with the colour of lapis or strong blue.

Lady Miriam - previous incarnations include that of Lady Guinivere and therefore is the soulmate of El Moraya. Represents alignment with the earth, magical innocence, goddess energy and the growth of civilisations through the connection and awareness of the earth energies.

Wottana - had incarnations during the times of the native American indians and therefore aligned closely to the earth. Focussed on shamanic practices, totem animals, humorous magical trickster, and medicine man. Linked to the colour of brown and turquoise and the smell of sage particularly when burnt as a smudge stick.

Lady Nightingale - Soulmate to Wottana, linked to the same colour of brown and totem animals. Again also quiet and earthy energy but brings with her connections through dreams and gentle awakenment to spiritual truth. Links with the smells of sage but also of Rosemary.

Kwan Yin - Worshipped as the Goddess of Compassion in China, represents powers of compassion, order and discipline. Colour linked to this Ascended Master is opalescent pearl and the smell of May Chang (an essential oil with a sweet and fruity fragrance).

Dwal Khul - Reputed to have written through Alice Bailey (a famous psychic) and is linked to Tibetan culture. Works through chaos leading to order. Seen as serene, smiling, quietly joyous as well as peaceful, can be called upon in cases of possession and demons. Works through the colour of Emerald Green and the smell of patchouli.

Serapis Bay - Seen as a bridge between the Ascended Masters and Archangels. Has links with Ancient Egypt and the lost civilisation of Atlantis. Oversees spiritual growth through grace and flow, helps to anchor the angelic influences and connections to the earth. Represented by the colour of opal and the smells of pine and the ocean.

There are other Ascended Masters who form the White Brotherhood or Lords and Ladies of Shambala, as they are also sometimes known. This is by no means a definitive list but as the earth is evolving they are drawing closer in order to provide us with their guidance and assistance during the times to come.

Conclusion

In conclusion, it may be worth considering just how little connection we now have with the cycles and energy of the earth.

Much of modern day living such as electricity, heating, cars and the ability to have whatever foods we desire with no regard to the season or parts of the world that we live in, has effectively caused us to lose the very skills and awareness' that enabled us to live and work within the constraints of the land we were born in.

Whilst there are not many people who would choose to exist in those undoubtedly hard times, we are now becoming increasingly aware of the need to respect and honour the earth in order to ensure that we do not destroy the very thing which allows us to live.

In accessing again the natural energy which surrounds us and encompasses our own being, we can create minor miracles in healing both ourselves and the earth every day of our lives.

My hope for this book is that everyone who reads it will find amongst its cover, at least one experience which opens them up to the world of possibility which is theirs.

In order to create miracles all any one of us ever needs is belief and faith in their own truth.

FREE DETAILED CATALOGUE

Capall Bann is owned and run by people actively involved in many of the areas in which we publish. A detailed illustrated catalogue is available on request, SAE or International Postal Coupon appreciated. **Titles can be ordered direct from Capall Bann, post free in the UK** (cheque or PO with order) or from good bookshops and specialist outlets.

Do contact us for details on the latest releases at: **Capall Bann Publishing, Freshfields, Chieveley, Berks, RG20 8TF.** Titles include:

Angels and Goddesses - Celtic Christianity & Paganism, M. Howard
Arthur - The Legend Unveiled, C Johnson & E Lung
Astrology The Inner Eye - A Guide in Everyday Language, E Smith
Auguries and Omens - The Magical Lore of Birds, Yvonne Aburrow
Asyniur - Womens Mysteries in the Northern Tradition, S McGrath
Beginnings - Geomancy, Builder's Rites & Electional Astrology in the
    European Tradition, Nigel Pennick
Between Earth and Sky, Julia Day
Book of the Veil , Peter Paddon
Caer Sidhe - Celtic Astrology and Astronomy, Vol 1, Michael Bayley
Call of the Horned Piper, Nigel Jackson
Cat's Company, Ann Walker
Celtic Faery Shamanism, Catrin James
Celtic Lore & Druidic Ritual, Rhiannon Ryall
Celtic Saints and the Glastonbury Zodiac, Mary Caine
Compleat Vampyre - The Vampyre Shaman, Nigel Jackson
Creating Form From the Mist - The Wisdom of Women in Celtic Myth and
    Culture, Lynne Sinclair-Wood
Crystal Clear - A Guide to Quartz Crystal, Jennifer Dent
Crystal Doorways, Simon & Sue Lilly
Dragons of the West, Nigel Pennick
Earth Dance - A Year of Pagan Rituals, Jan Brodie
Earth Harmony - Places of Power, Holiness & Healing, Nigel Pennick
Earth Magic, Margaret McArthur
Enchanted Forest - The Magical Lore of Trees, Yvonne Aburrow
Eternally Yours Faithfully, Roy Radford & Evelyn Gregory
Everything You Always Wanted To Know About Your Body, But So Far
    Nobody's Been Able To Tell You, Chris Thomas & D Baker
Face of the Deep - Healing Body & Soul, Penny Allen
Fairies in the Irish Tradition, Molly Gowen
Familiars - Animal Powers of Britain, Anna Franklin

Fool's First Steps, (The) Chris Thomas
Forest Paths - Tree Divination, Brian Harrison, Ill. S. Rouse
From Past to Future Life, Dr Roger Webber
Gardening For Wildlife Ron Wilson
Handbook For Pagan Healers, Liz Joan
Handbook of Fairies, Ronan Coghlan
Healing Book, The, Chris Thomas and Diane Baker
Healing Homes, Jennifer Dent
Healing Journeys, Paul Williamson
Healing Stones, Sue Philips
Herb Craft - Shamanic & Ritual Use of Herbs, Lavender & Franklin
In Search of Herne the Hunter, Eric Fitch
Inner Space Workbook - Develop Thru Tarot, C Summers & J Vayne
Intuitive Journey, Ann Walker Isis - African Queen, Akkadia Ford
Journey Home, The, Chris Thomas
Language of the Psycards, Berenice
Legend of Robin Hood, The, Richard Rutherford-Moore
Living Tarot, Ann Walker
Lore of the Sacred Horse, Marion Davies
Magic of Herbs - A Complete Home Herbal, Rhiannon Ryall
Magical Guardians - Exploring the Spirit and Nature of Trees, Philip Heselton
Magical History of the Horse, Janet Farrar & Virginia Russell
Magical Lore of Animals, Yvonne Aburrow
Magical Lore of Cats, Marion Davies
Magical Lore of Herbs, Marion Davies
Magick Without Peers, Ariadne Rainbird & David Rankine
Masks of Misrule - Horned God & His Cult in Europe, Nigel Jackson
Medicine For The Coming Age, Lisa Sand MD
Medium Rare - Reminiscences of a Clairvoyant, Muriel Renard
Menopausal Woman on the Run, Jaki da Costa
Mind Massage - 60 Creative Visualisations, Marlene Maundrill
Moon Mysteries, Jan Brodie
Mystic Life of Animals, Ann Walker
New Celtic Oracle The, Nigel Pennick & Nigel Jackson
Pagan Feasts - Seasonal Food for the 8 Festivals, Franklin & Phillips
Patchwork of Magic - Living in a Pagan World, Julia Day
Pathworking - A Practical Book of Guided Meditations, Pete Jennings
Personal Power, Anna Franklin
Places of Pilgrimage and Healing, Adrian Cooper
Practical Divining, Richard Foord
Practical Meditation, Steve Hounsome
Practical Spirituality, Steve Hounsome
Psychic Self Defence - Real Solutions, Jan Brodie
Real Fairies, David Tame
Reality - How It Works & Why It Mostly Doesn't, Rik Dent
Romany Tapestry, Michael Houghton

Sacred Animals, Gordon MacLellan
Sacred Celtic Animals, Marion Davies, Ill. Simon Rouse
Sacred Dorset - On the Path of the Dragon, Peter Knight
Sacred Grove - The Mysteries of the Forest, Yvonne Aburrow
Sacred Geometry, Nigel Pennick
Sacred Nature, Ancient Wisdom & Modern Meanings, A Cooper
Sacred Ring - Pagan Origins of British Folk Festivals, M. Howard
Season of Sorcery - On Becoming a Wisewoman, Poppy Palin
Seasonal Magic - Diary of a Village Witch, Paddy Slade
Secret Places of the Goddess, Philip Heselton
Secret Signs & Sigils, Nigel Pennick
Self Enlightenment, Mayan O'Brien
Spirits of the Earth series, Jaq D Hawkins
Stony Gaze, Investigating Celtic Heads John Billingsley
Stumbling Through the Undergrowth , Mark Kirwan-Heyhoe
Symbols of Ancient Gods, Rhiannon Ryall
Talking to the Earth, Gordon MacLellan
Taming the Wolf - Full Moon Meditations, Steve Hounsome
Teachings of the Wisewomen, Rhiannon Ryall
The Other Kingdoms Speak, Helena Hawley
Tree: Essence of Healing, Simon & Sue Lilly
Tree: Essence, Spirit & Teacher, Simon & Sue Lilly
Through the Veil, Peter Paddon
Understanding Chaos Magic, Jaq D Hawkins
Vortex - The End of History, Mary Russell
Warp and Weft - In Search of the I-Ching, William de Fancourt
Warriors at the Edge of Time, Jan Fry
Water Witches, Tony Steele
Way of the Magus, Michael Howard
Weaving a Web of Magic, Rhiannon Ryall
West Country Wicca, Rhiannon Ryall
Wildwitch - The Craft of the Natural Psychic, Poppy Palin
Wildwood King , Philip Kane
Wondrous Land - The Faery Faith of Ireland by Dr Kay Mullin
Working With the Merlin, Geoff Hughes
Your Talking Pet, Ann Walker

FREE detailed catalogue and FREE 'Inspiration' magazine
Contact: Capall Bann Publishing, Freshfields, Chieveley, Berks, RG20 8TF